Wok Recipes

An Easy Wok Cookbook for Stir Fries

By
BookSumo Press

Published by
http://www.booksumo.com

LEGAL NOTES

Table of Contents

Tropical Chicken Stir Fry 9

Coconut Zesty Chicken Stir Fry 10

Nutty Chicken and Carrot Stir Fry 11

Zucchini Broccoli Stir Fry 12

Pecan Chicken Stir Fry 13

Cabbage Chicken Stir Fry 14

Chili and Sweet Chicken Stir Fry 15

Herbed Coconut Chicken Stir Fry 16

Chow Mein Chicken Stir Fry 17

Bangkok Curry Stir Fry 18

Fruity Veggies and Chicken Stir Fry 19

Spinach and Chicken Stir Fry 20

Canola Mushroom Chicken Stir Fry 21

Tamari Veggies and Chicken Stir Fry 22

Ramen Chicken Stir Fry 23

Chicken and Tofu Clash Stir Fry 24

Sweet Pineapple and Apricot Chicken Stir Fry 25

Ginger Chicken Stir Fry 26

Scallion Mushroom Chicken Stir Fry 27

Honey Chicken Stir Fry 28

Spicy Mustard Chicken Stir Fry 29

Popping Teriyaki Chicken Stir Fry 30

Classic Paprika Chicken Fry 31

Teriyaki Chicken Stir Fry with Noodles 32

Grilled Chicken Stir Fry Linguine 33

Tangerine Chicken Stir Fry 34

Basmati Chicken Stir Fry Spears 36

Beachy Chicken Stir Fry 37

Fried Teriyaki Chicken Rice 38

American Parsley Chicken Stir Fry 39

Creamy Canola Chicken Stir Fry 40

Chipotle Chicken Stir Fry 41

Cashew Chicken Breasts Stir Fry 42

Teriyaki Chicken Tortellini Stir Fry 43

Summer Chicken Stir Fry 44

Roasted Nutty Chicken Stir Fry 45

Spicy Chicken Noodles Stir Fry 46

Spicy Chestnut Chicken Stir Fry 47

Carrot, Cabbage, and Chicken Wok 48

Sweet and Salty Chicken Stir Fry 49

Chili Fried Chicken Breast Bites 50

Wild Hoisin Chicken Stir Fry 51

Plum Peanut and Chicken Stir Fry 52

Beginners' Creamy Chicken Stir Fry 53

Italian Bell Chicken Stir Fry 54

Oriental Chili Chicken and Ramen Stir Fry 55

Corny Grilled Chicken Stir Fry 56

Peanut Butter Chicken Stir Fry 57

A Texas-Mexican Stir Fry 58

Grapes and Chicken Wok 59

Tofu and Miso 60

Teriyaki Chicken Rice Stir Fry 61

Tilapia Fillets with Teriyaki Sauce 62

Glazed Salmon Fillets with Orzo 63

Teriyaki Burgers 64

Beef Stir-Fry 65

Ramen Sesame Soup 66

Japanese Dashi Omelet 67

Hawaiian Ramen Wok 68

Sweet Ramen with Tofu 69

Ginger Beef Ramen 70

Louisiana x Japan Ramen 71

American Ground Beef Ramen 72

Tipsy Japanese Crumbled Beef 73

Savory and Sweet Omelet 74

Tropical Curry Ramen 75

Japanese Sweet Chicken Stir Fry 76

Japanese Sesame Egg Sushi 77

$3 Dollar Dinner 78

Sweet and Spicy Ramen Stir Fry 79

Ramen Steak Wok 80

Japanese Spring Stir Fry 81

Japanese Fruity Chicken Curry 82

Ramen Green Bean Stir Fry 83

Japanese Chicken Thighs Wok 84

Apple Ramen Salad 85

Mung Bang Noodles Wok 86

Hawaiian Fried Rice II 87

Fried Rice Cauliflower 88

Curried Apple and Raisins Fried Rice 89

Seafood Sampler Fried Rice 90

Creamy Corn Soup 91

Ginger Chili Plum Steak 92

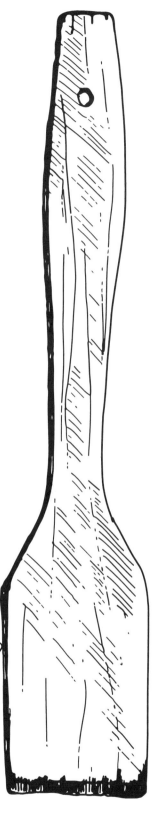

Beef and Broccoli I 93

Pineapple Pepper Curry 94

Halibut BBQ Tacos 95

Chicken Tikka Masala 96

Garlic and Lime Shrimp Wok 98

Pan Seared Halibut Cambodia 99

Pink and Green Stir Fry 100

Catfish Skillet 101

Eggplants in Ginger Vinaigrette Glaze 102

Hot and Spicy Seafood Filets 103

Khmer Shrimp Wok 104

Apricot and Asparagus Wok 105

Cambodian Breakfast Frittatas 106

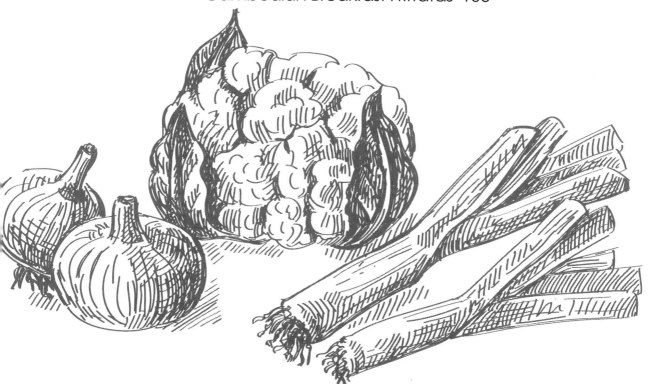

Tropical Chicken Stir Fry

🥣 Prep Time: 10 mins

🕐 Total Time: 40 mins

Servings per Recipe: 6

Calories	238 kcal
Fat	7.7 g
Carbohydrates	21g
Protein	20.2 g
Cholesterol	44 mg
Sodium	412 mg

Ingredients

1/4 C. reduced-salt soy sauce
2 tbsp white wine vinegar
2 tbsp mirin (sweetened Asian wine)
1 tsp grated ginger root
2 crushed garlic cloves
1 tbsp cornstarch
2 tbsp oil, preferably sesame oil
1 lb boneless, skinless chicken breast, cut in 1-inch pieces

6 large green onions, cut in 1-inch pieces
2 C. fresh or frozen pepper strips
1 (20 oz) can chunk pineapple in juice
1/4 C. sliced almonds (optional)

Directions

1. Get a small mixing bowl: Whisk in it the soy sauce with mirin, vinegar, ginger, cornstarch and garlic.
2. Place a large wok over medium heat. Heat the oil in it. Cook in it the chicken for 6 min. Drain it and place it aside.
3. Stir the green onions, peppers and pineapple to the wok and cook them for 4 min.
4. Stir in the back the chicken and cook them for another 4 min. Serve your stir fry warm.
5. Enjoy.

COCONUT
Zesty Chicken Stir Fry

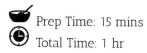

Prep Time: 15 mins
Total Time: 1 hr

Servings per Recipe: 4
Calories	660 kcal
Fat	31.2 g
Carbohydrates	53g
Protein	43.8 g
Cholesterol	104 mg
Sodium	117 mg

Ingredients

1 1/2 lb skinless, boneless chicken breast halves - cut into 1 inch cubes
2 limes, zested and juiced
2 tbsp grated fresh ginger root
1 3/4 C. coconut milk
1/2 tsp white sugar
1 C. jasmine rice

1 tbsp sesame oil
1 tbsp honey
1/4 C. sweetened flaked coconut

Directions

1. Get a large mixing bowl: Combine in it the chicken breast cubes with lime juice, lime zest, and grated ginger. Stir them. Place the mix aside for 22 min.
2. Place a small saucepan over medium heat. Stir in the coconut milk and sugar. Cook them until they start simmering. Add the rice. Lower the heat and cook them for 22 min.
3. Place a large wok over medium heat. Heat the oil in it. Stir in the chicken with marinade. Cook them for 4 min.
4. Add the honey and cook them for 2 min. Drain the rice and place it aside to cool down slightly.
5. Serve your honey chicken with rice and coconut flakes warm.
6. Enjoy.

Nutty Chicken and Carrot Stir Fry

Prep Time: 10 mins
Total Time: 20 mins

Servings per Recipe: 6
Calories	235 kcal
Fat	7.9 g
Carbohydrates	12.9 g
Protein	27.4 g
Cholesterol	69 mg
Sodium	529 mg

Ingredients

2 tsp peanut oil
2 stalks celery, chopped
2 carrots, peeled and diagonally sliced
1 1/2 lb skinless, boneless chicken breast halves - cut into strips
1 tbsp cornstarch
3/4 C. orange juice
3 tbsp light soy sauce
1 tbsp honey
1 tsp minced fresh ginger root
1/4 C. cashews
1/4 C. minced green onions

Directions

1. Place a large wok over medium heat. Heat 1 teaspoon of oil in it.
2. Cook in it the celery with carrot for 4 min. Stir in the remaining oil with chicken then cook them for 6 min.
3. Get a small mixing bowl: Whisk in it the orange juice with cornstarch. Add the soy sauce, honey and ginger then whisk them to make the sauce.
4. Stir the sauce to the wok and cook them until the sauce becomes thick. Serve your chicken stir fry warm with some cashews and green onions.
5. Enjoy.

ZUCCHINI
Broccoli Stir Fry

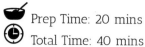 Prep Time: 20 mins
Total Time: 40 mins

Servings per Recipe: 2
Calories	313 kcal
Fat	16.1 g
Carbohydrates	20.1g
Protein	22.1 g
Cholesterol	45 mg
Sodium	1214 mg

Ingredients

6 oz skinless, boneless chicken breast,
cut into small pieces
2 tbsp soy sauce
2 tbsp dry sherry
1 tbsp cornstarch
1 tbsp vegetable oil
1 C. broccoli florets, cut into pieces

1 large green bell pepper, cut into squares
1 zucchini, cut into rounds and quartered
3 cloves garlic, minced
1/2 C. chicken broth
1 tbsp vegetable oil
6 green onions, chopped

Directions

1. Get a large mixing bowl: Toss in it the chicken, soy sauce, sherry, and cornstarch.
2. Place a large wok over medium heat. Heat 1 tbsp of oil in it. Add the broccoli, bell pepper, zucchini, and garlic. Cook them for 4 min.
3. Stir in the broth and put on the lid. Cook them for 7 min. Transfer the mix to a bowl and place it aside.
4. Place a large wok over medium heat. Heat in it the rest of oil. Add the chicken with a pinch of salt and pepper for 7 min.
5. Add the cooked veggies mix. Cook them for 4 min. Serve your stir fry warm.
6. Enjoy.

Pecan
Chicken Stir Fry

Prep Time: 15 mins
Total Time: 35 mins

Servings per Recipe: 4
Calories	312 kcal
Fat	17.2 g
Carbohydrates	11.1g
Protein	30 g
Cholesterol	72 mg
Sodium	87 mg

Ingredients

1 tbsp extra virgin olive oil
4 skinless, boneless chicken breast halves
- cut into strips
1 C. julienned carrots
1 small onion, chopped
1 zucchini squash, peeled and cut into 1 inch rounds

1 C. fresh sliced mushrooms
2 yellow summer squash, peeled and sliced into 1 inch pieces
1/2 C. pecan halves
1 tsp coarse ground black pepper

Directions

1. Place a large wok over medium heat. Grease it with oil. Add the chicken and cook it for 4 min.
2. Stir in the onion with carrot. Cook them for 4 min. Stir in the mushrooms, zucchini, and squash then cook them for 6 to 8 min.
3. Season them with some salt and pepper then cook them for 4 min. Serve your stir fry warm.
4. Enjoy.

CABBAGE
Chicken Stir Fry

Prep Time: 20 mins
Total Time: 1 hr 10 mins

Servings per Recipe: 4

Calories	337 kcal
Fat	8.6 g
Carbohydrates	32.3g
Protein	31.7 g
Cholesterol	67 mg
Sodium	1364 mg

Ingredients

2 tbsp peanut oil
6 cloves garlic, minced
1 tsp grated fresh ginger
1 bunch green onions, chopped
1 tsp salt
1 lb boneless skinless chicken breasts,
cut into strips
2 onions, thinly sliced
1 C. sliced cabbage

1 red bell pepper, thinly sliced
2 C. sugar snap peas
1 C. chicken broth
2 tbsp soy sauce
2 tbsp white sugar
2 tbsp cornstarch

Directions

1. Place a large wok over medium heat. Heat the oil in it and cook in it 2 cloves of garlic, ginger root, green onions and salt for 3 min.
2. Stir in the chicken for 4 min. Stir in the rest of the garlic with sweet onions, cabbage, bell pepper, peas and 1/2 C. of the broth/water. Put on the lid and let them simmer.
3. Get a small bowl: Whisk in it the 1/2 C. broth/water, soy sauce, sugar and cornstarch to make the sauce.
4. Stir the sauce into the wok and cook them until the sauce becomes thick. Serve your stir fry right away with some white rice.
5. Enjoy.

Chili
and Sweet Chicken Stir Fry

Prep Time: 10 mins
Total Time: 30 mins

Servings per Recipe: 4
Calories	156 kcal
Fat	6.2 g
Carbohydrates	10.9 g
Protein	15.9 g
Cholesterol	36 mg
Sodium	606 mg

Ingredients

3 C. broccoli florets
1 tbsp olive oil
2 skinless, boneless chicken breast halves
- cut into 1 inch strips
1/4 C. sliced green onions
4 cloves garlic, thinly sliced
1 tbsp hoisin sauce
1 tbsp chile paste
1 tbsp low sodium soy sauce

1/2 tsp ground ginger
1/4 tsp crushed red pepper
1/2 tsp salt
1/2 tsp black pepper
1/8 C. chicken stock

Directions

1. Steam the broccoli florets for 6 min.
2. Place a large wok over medium heat. Heat the oil in it. Add the chicken with green onions, and garlic. Cook them for 6 min.
3. Add the remaining ingredients except for the broccoli and cook them for 3 min. Stir in the steamed broccoli and cook them for 2 min.
4. Serve your Stir fry with some white rice.
5. Enjoy.

HERBED
Coconut Chicken Stir Fry

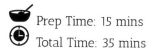

Prep Time: 15 mins
Total Time: 35 mins

Servings per Recipe: 6

Calories	506 kcal
Fat	12.1 g
Carbohydrates	60g
Protein	36.9 g
Cholesterol	78 mg
Sodium	804 mg

Ingredients

2 C. uncooked jasmine rice
1 quart water
3/4 C. coconut milk
3 tbsp soy sauce
3 tbsp rice wine vinegar
1 1/2 tbsp fish sauce
3/4 tsp red pepper flakes
1 tbsp olive oil
1 medium onion, sliced

2 tbsp fresh ginger root, minced
3 cloves garlic, minced
2 lb skinless, boneless chicken breast
halves - cut into 1/2 inch strips
3 shiitake mushrooms, sliced
5 green onions, chopped
1 1/2 C. chopped fresh basil leaves

Directions

1. Cook the rice according to the directions on the package.
2. Get a mixing bowl: Whisk in it the coconut milk, soy sauce, rice wine vinegar, fish sauce, and red pepper flakes.
3. Place a large wok over medium heat: heat the oil in it. Cook in it the onion, ginger, and garlic. Add chicken and cook them for 4 min.
4. Add the coconut milk and coco the sauce until it lowers by 1/3 of it. Add the mushrooms, green onions, and basil. Coo them for 3 min. Serve your stir fry warm with some rice.
5. Enjoy.

Chow Mein
Chicken Stir Fry

Prep Time: 10 mins
Total Time: 45 mins

Servings per Recipe: 4
Calories	524 kcal
Fat	25.1 g
Carbohydrates	41.1g
Protein	34.7 g
Cholesterol	68 mg
Sodium	1749 mg

Ingredients

1 C. orange juice
1 tbsp grated orange zest
1/4 C. soy sauce
1 tsp salt
3 cloves garlic, chopped
1 tbsp brown sugar
3 tbsp vegetable oil
4 skinless, boneless chicken breast halves
- cut into 1 inch cubes

2 tbsp all-purpose flour
1 C. bean sprouts (optional)
1 (6 oz) package crispy chow mein noodles

Directions

1. Get a small mixing bowl: Whisk in it the juice, orange zest, soy sauce, salt, garlic and brown sugar to make the sauce.
2. Place a large wok over medium heat. Heat the oil in it. Cook in it the chicken for 9 min. Stir in the sauce until it starts boiling.
3. Sprinkle the flour on top. Cook the stir fry until it becomes thick. Stir in the bean sprouts and cook them for 2 min.
4. Serve your stir fry warm with the chow mein noodles.
5. Enjoy

BANGKOK
Curry Stir Fry

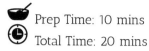 Prep Time: 10 mins
Total Time: 20 mins

Servings per Recipe: 4
Calories	271 kcal
Fat	15.8 g
Carbohydrates	11.2g
Protein	25.4 g
Cholesterol	59 mg
Sodium	147 mg

Ingredients

2 tsp olive oil
1 lb skinless, boneless chicken breast
halves - cut into thin strips
1 tbsp Thai red curry paste
1 C. sliced halved zucchini
1 red bell pepper, seeded and sliced into
strips
1/2 C. sliced carrots
1 onion, quartered then halved

1 tbsp cornstarch
1 (14 oz) can light coconut milk
2 tbsp chopped fresh cilantro

Directions

1. Place a large wok over medium heat. Heat the oil in it. Cook in it the chicken for 4 min.
2. Stir in the curry paste, zucchini, bell pepper, carrot and onion then cook them for 4 min.
3. Get a small mixing bowl: Whisk in it the cornstarch with coconut milk. Stir the mix into the wok. Cook the stir fry until it starts boiling.
4. Lower the heat and cook the stir fry for 2 min. Serve it warm.
5. Enjoy.

Fruity Veggies and Chicken Stir Fry

Prep Time: 20 mins
Total Time: 40 mins

Servings per Recipe: 4
Calories   380 kcal
Fat   14 g
Carbohydrates   33.1g
Protein   31.7 g
Cholesterol   68 mg
Sodium   938 mg

Ingredients

1/2 C. orange juice
3 tbsp soy sauce
3 cloves garlic, chopped
1 tbsp grated orange zest
1 tsp ground ginger
1/2 tsp red pepper flakes (optional)
3 tbsp vegetable oil
4 skinless, boneless chicken breast halves, thinly sliced

1/2 C. chicken broth
2 tbsp cornstarch
1 (16 oz) package frozen stir-fry vegetables
1 C. sugar snap peas
1 C. broccoli florets
1 C. sliced carrot

Directions

1. Get a small mixing bowl: Whisk in it the orange juice, soy sauce, garlic, orange zest, ground ginger, and red pepper flakes to make the sauce.
2. Place a large wok over medium heat. Heat the oil in it. Stir into it the sauce with chicken. Cook them for 12 min.
3. Get a small mixing bowl: Whisk the broth with cornstarch in it. Add the mix the mix then cook it until it becomes thick.
4. Stir in the veggies and cook them for 12 min. Serve your stir fry warm.
5. Enjoy.

SPINACH
and Chicken Stir Fry

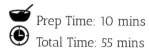 Prep Time: 10 mins

Total Time: 55 mins

Servings per Recipe: 6	
Calories	278 kcal
Fat	13 g
Carbohydrates	5.9 g
Protein	33.8 g
Cholesterol	86 mg
Sodium	273 mg

Ingredients

1 tbsp soy sauce
2 tbsp water
1 tbsp white sugar
2 lb skinless, boneless chicken breast
halves, cut into small pieces
1 tbsp vegetable oil
5 green onions, sliced
3 cloves garlic, chopped
3 tbsp vegetable oil

2 (6 oz) bags fresh baby spinach leaves
1 C. thinly sliced fresh basil

Directions

1. Get large mixing bowl: Whisk in it the soy sauce, water, and sugar. Toss in it the chicken and place it aside for 35.
2. Place a large wok over medium heat. Heat 1 tbsp of oil in it. Cook in it the green onion with garlic for 2 min. Drain the mix and place it aside.
3. Heat 3 tbsp of oil in the same pan. Cook in it the chicken with marinade for 6 min.
4. Stir in the spinach and put on the lid. Cook them for 5 min while stirring them from time to time.
5. Add the cooked onion and garlic mix. Cook them for 3 min. Add the basil and cook them for another 3 min. Serve your stir fry warm.
6. Enjoy.

Canola
Mushroom Chicken Stir Fry

🥣 Prep Time: 20 mins
🕐 Total Time: 40 mins

Servings per Recipe: 4
Calories	190 kcal
Fat	6.3 g
Carbohydrates	8.7g
Protein	25.8 g
Cholesterol	59 mg
Sodium	600 mg

Ingredients

1/2 large eggplant, sliced into rounds
1/8 tsp salt
4 skinless, boneless chicken breast halves, cut into cubes
2 cloves garlic, minced
2 tbsp soy sauce

1 tbsp canola oil
2 C. mushrooms, sliced
1/8 tsp ground black pepper
4 C. spinach

Directions

1. Season the eggplant slices with some salt. Place them aside to sit for 6 min. Cut them into the dices.
2. Place a large wok over heat and grease it with some oil. Add with chicken, garlic, and soy sauce. Cook them for 12 min.
3. Add the mushroom with black pepper. Cook them for 4 min.
4. Place another wok over medium heat. Heat the canola oil in it. Cook the eggplant until it becomes golden brown.
5. Transfer the eggplant to the chicken stir fry with spinach and cook them for 4 min. Serve your stir fry warm.
6. Enjoy.

TAMARI
Veggies and Chicken Stir Fry

 Prep Time: 15 mins

Total Time: 1 hr

Servings per Recipe: 4

Calories	849 kcal
Fat	17.5 g
Carbohydrates	112.5g
Protein	67.6 g
Cholesterol	129 mg
Sodium	1838 mg

Ingredients

1 (16 oz) package dry whole-wheat
noodles
1/2 C. chicken stock
1/2 C. orange marmalade
1/3 C. tamari sauce
1 (1 inch) piece ginger root, peeled
ground black pepper to taste
1 lemon, juiced
3 tbsp peanut oil

2 lb skinless, boneless chicken breast
halves, cut into thin strips
1 (16 oz) bag frozen stir-fry vegetables,
thawed

Directions

1. Cook the noodles according to the directions on the package. Remove it from the water and place it aside.
2. Place a large saucepan over medium heat. Stir in it the stock, orange marmalade, tamari sauce, whole ginger root piece, and ground black pepper to make the sauce.
3. Cook them until they start boiling. Lower the heat and cook the sauce until it becomes thick for 22 min.
4. Turn off the heat and add the lemon juice. Place the sauce aside.
5. Place a large wok or wok over medium heat. Heat the oil in it. Cook in it the chicken for 8 min. Drain it and place it aside.
6. Add the veggies to the wok and cook them for 6 min. Discard the ginger root. Add the chicken back with sauce and stir them. Cook them for 3 min.
7. Serve your chicken stir fry with noodles warm.
8. Enjoy.

Ramen
Chicken Stir Fry

Prep Time: 15 mins
Total Time: 30 mins

Servings per Recipe: 8
Calories	263 kcal
Fat	9 g
Carbohydrates	31g
Protein	14.3 g
Cholesterol	27 mg
Sodium	695 mg

Ingredients

3 tbsp vegetable oil
3 skinless, boneless chicken breast halves
- cut into strips
2 stalks celery, chopped
2 zucchini, quartered and sliced
10 mushrooms, sliced
2 C. chopped spinach
1 (3 oz) package ramen noodle pasta with
flavor packet

1 C. uncooked long-grain rice
1 tbsp cornstarch
1/4 C. cold water
1 tsp vegetable oil
1/4 C. soy sauce

Directions

1. Place a large wok over medium heat. Heat the oil in it. Cook in it the chicken for 8 min.
2. Add the celery with zucchini and cook them for 4 min. Stir in the spinach with mushroom and cook them for 3 min.
3. Lower the heat and keep them cooking while stirring from time to time.
4. Cook the rice and ramen noodles according to the instructions on the packages. Drain them and place them aside.
5. Get a small mixing bowl: Whisk in it the cornstarch, water, oil and soy sauce. Stir the mix into the wok with the veggies. Add the noodles and rice then toss them to coat.
6. Cook them for 6 min. Serve your stir fry right away.
7. Enjoy.

CHICKEN
and Tofu Clash Stir Fry

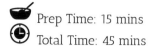

Prep Time: 15 mins
Total Time: 45 mins

Servings per Recipe: 6
Calories	172 kcal
Fat	6.4 g
Carbohydrates	11.8g
Protein	17.8 g
Cholesterol	20 mg
Sodium	548 mg

Ingredients

3 tbsp light soy sauce
1 tsp white sugar
1 tbsp cornstarch
3 tbsp Chinese rice wine
1 medium green onion, diced
2 skinless, boneless chicken breast halves - cut into bite-size pieces
3 cloves garlic, chopped
1 yellow onion, thinly sliced

2 green bell peppers, thinly sliced
1 (12 oz) package firm tofu, drained and cubed
1/2 C. water
2 tbsp oyster sauce
1 1/2 tbsp chili paste with garlic

Directions

1. Get a mixing bowl: Combine in it the soy sauce, sugar, cornstarch, and rice wine. Whisk them well. Stir in the chicken with onion. Place them aside for 17 min.
2. Place a large wok over medium heat and grease it with oil. Cook in the chicken and onion with the marinade for 6 min.
3. Add the garlic, onion, and peppers. Cook them for 6 min. Stir in the tofu, water, oyster sauce, and chili paste.
4. Cook them for 5 min while stirring often. Serve your stir fry warm.
5. Enjoy.

Sweet Pineapple and Apricot Chicken Stir Fry

Prep Time: 25 mins

Total Time: 40 mins

Servings per Recipe: 6	
Calories	220 kcal
Fat	6.6 g
Carbohydrates	23.2g
Protein	18.7 g
Cholesterol	43 mg
Sodium	529 mg

Ingredients

1 (15 oz) can apricot halves, drained and chopped, juice reserved
2 tbsp soy sauce
1 tbsp cornstarch
1/2 tsp garlic powder
1/2 tsp onion powder
1/2 tsp crushed red pepper flakes
2 tbsp vegetable oil
1 tbsp minced fresh ginger root

1 lb skinless, boneless chicken breast meat - cut into strips
1 (16 oz) package frozen stir-fry vegetables, thawed
1 (8 oz) can pineapple chunks, drained
3 green onion, sliced

Directions

1. Get a mixing bowl: Mix in it the apricot juice, soy sauce, cornstarch, garlic powder, onion powder, and red pepper flakes. Add the cornstarch and mix them well to make the sauce.

2. Place a large wok or wok over medium heat. Heat the oil in it. Add the ginger and cook it for 15 sec. Stir in the chicken and cook it for 8 min.

3. Add the veggies and cook them for 6 to 8 min. Add the apricots, pineapple chunks, and sauce. Cook the stir fry for 2 min. Fold in the green onion then serve it warm.

4. Enjoy.

GINGER
Chicken Stir Fry

Prep Time: 15 mins
Total Time: 25 mins

Servings per Recipe: 4

Calories	222 kcal
Fat	10.5 g
Carbohydrates	10.7g
Protein	20.7 g
Cholesterol	55 mg
Sodium	389 mg

Ingredients

3 skinless, boneless chicken breast
halves
1 (2 inch) piece fresh ginger root
2 tbsp coconut oil

2 1/2 tsp pressed garlic
1/3 C. hoisin sauce

Directions

1. Cut the chicken breasts into strips and place them aside. Remove the peel of the ginger root and grate it.
2. Place a large wok over medium heat. Heat the coconut oil in it. Add the garlic with ginger and cook them for 30 sec.
3. Stir in the chicken with hoisin sauce and cook them for 8 min. Serve your stir fry warm.
4. Enjoy.

Scallion Mushroom Chicken Stir Fry

Prep Time: 10 mins
Total Time: 40 mins

Servings per Recipe: 4
Calories	256 kcal
Fat	7.7 g
Carbohydrates	16.5g
Protein	31.1 g
Cholesterol	70 mg
Sodium	614 mg

Ingredients

1 lemon
1/2 C. reduced sodium chicken broth
3 tbsp reduced-sodium soy sauce
2 tsp cornstarch
1 lb boneless skinless chicken breasts, trimmed and cut into 1-inch pieces
10 oz mushrooms, halved or quartered
1 C. diagonally sliced carrots (1/4-inch thick)

1 tbsp canola oil
2 C. snow peas, stem and strings removed
1 bunch scallions, cut into 1-inch pieces, white and green parts divided
1 tbsp chopped garlic

Directions

1. Reserve 1 tbsp of grated lemon zest from the lemon.
2. Get a mixing bowl: Whisk in it 3 tbsp of the juice with broth, soy sauce and cornstarch.
3. Place a wok or wok over medium heat. Heat the oil in it. Brown in it the chicken for 6 min. Drain it and place it aside.
4. Stir in the mushroom with carrot and cook them for 6 min. Stir in the snow peas, scallion whites, garlic and lemon zest. Cook them for 30 sec.
5. Stir in the lemon juice mix and cook them for 4 min until the sauce becomes thick. Stir in the scallions with cooked chicken. Cook them for 3 min then serve it warm.
6. Enjoy.

HONEY
Chicken Stir Fry

Prep Time: 15 mins
Total Time: 30 mins

Servings per Recipe: 5
Calories	720 kcal
Fat	40.3 g
Carbohydrates	35g
Protein	52.6 g
Cholesterol	347 mg
Sodium	290 mg

Ingredients

1/3 C. sweetened condensed milk
1/3 C. mayonnaise
1 tsp white sugar
2 tsp white vinegar
2 tsp honey
2 lb skinless, boneless chicken breast
halves - diced

6 eggs, beaten
1 C. all-purpose flour
1/3 C. canola oil

Directions

1. Get a small mixing bowl: Whisk in it the condensed milk, mayonnaise, sugar, vinegar, and honey to make the sauce. Place it aside.
2. Get a large mixing bowl: Toss in it the chicken with eggs. Drain the chicken dices and dust them with the flour.
3. Place a large work or wok over medium heat. Heat the oil in it. Brown in it the chicken for 3 min. Add the sauce and cook them for 17 min until the chicken is cooked and the sauce is thick.
4. Serve your stir fry warm.
5. Enjoy.

Spicy Mustard Chicken Stir Fry

🥣 Prep Time: 15 mins
🕐 Total Time: 45 mins

Servings per Recipe: 4
Calories	584 kcal
Fat	15.5 g
Carbohydrates	95g
Protein	17.9 g
Cholesterol	40 mg
Sodium	769 mg

Ingredients

4 C. water
1/4 tsp salt
2 tbsp butter
3 dried red chiles, broken into several pieces
2 C. uncooked white rice
1 tbsp sesame oil
2 garlic cloves, minced
2 tbsp soy sauce, divided
1 skinless, boneless chicken breast half, diced
1 tsp dried basil

1 tsp ground white pepper
1/2 tsp dry ground mustard
1 pinch ground turmeric
1 tbsp butter
1 1/2 C. broccoli florets
1 C. diced green bell pepper
1 C. diced red bell pepper
1/2 C. diced onion
1 tsp lemon juice

Directions

1. Place a medium saucepan over medium heat. Stir in it the water, salt, 2 tbsp butter, and red chili peppers. Cook them until they start boiling.
2. Add the rice and put on lid. Cook it for 22 min over medium heat while stirring it from time to time.
3. Place a large wok over medium heat. Heat the oil in it. Cook in it the garlic for 2 min.
4. Stir in the half of the soy sauce with chicken, basil, white pepper, dry mustard, and turmeric with garlic. Cook them for 9 min. Stir in the remaining soy sauce.
5. Place another wok or wok over medium heat. Heat 1 tbsp of butter in it. Cook in it the broccoli, green pepper, red pepper, and onion for 12 min.
6. Add the lemon juice and toss them. Stir the veggies into the chicken stir fry. Serve them warm.
7. Enjoy.

POPPING
Teriyaki Chicken Stir Fry

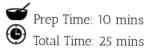 Prep Time: 10 mins
Total Time: 25 mins

Servings per Recipe: 4
Calories	208 kcal
Fat	9.7 g
Carbohydrates	14.1g
Protein	17.1 g
Cholesterol	36 mg
Sodium	1432 mg

Ingredients

2 tsp ground ginger
2 tbsp soy sauce
1 tsp rice vinegar
3 tbsp teriyaki sauce
2 tsp ground black pepper
2 tsp poppy seeds
2 tbsp sesame oil

2 cloves garlic, minced
1/2 large onion, quartered
2 skinless, boneless chicken breast halves,
cut into 1-inch pieces
1 (16 oz) bag fresh stir-fry vegetables

Directions

1. Get a mixing bowl: Mix in it the ginger, soy sauce, rice vinegar, teriyaki sauce, black pepper, and poppy seeds to make the sauce.
2. Place a large wok over medium heat. Heat the oil in it. Add the onion with garlic and cook them for 4 min.
3. Stir in the chicken and cook them for 6 min. Stir in the teriyaki sauce. Cook them until they start boiling. Add the veggies and cook them for 8 min.
4. Serve your stir fry right away with some white rice.
5. Enjoy.

Classic
Paprika Chicken Fry

Prep Time: 25 mins
Total Time: 45 mins

Servings per Recipe: 4
Calories	223 kcal
Fat	7.1 g
Carbohydrates	13.1g
Protein	28.4 g
Cholesterol	67 mg
Sodium	1443 mg

Ingredients

1 tbsp flaked sea salt
2 tsp finely cracked black pepper
1 tsp crushed red pepper flakes, or to taste
1 tsp Chinese five-spice powder
1 tsp ground paprika
4 skinless, boneless chicken breast halves
-- trimmed and cut into quarters

1 tbsp vegetable oil
1 lb broccoli florets, cut in half
3 small carrots, peeled and cut into
matchstick-sized pieces

Directions

1. Get a small mixing bowl: Combine in it the sea salt, black pepper, red pepper flakes, five-spice powder, and paprika. Mix them well.

2. Place a large wok over medium heat. Heat the oil in it. Massage the spice mix into the chicken and brown it for 12 min on each side.

3. Add the carrot with broccoli. Cook them for 14 min while stirring often. Serve your stir fry warm.

4. Enjoy.

TERIYAKI
Chicken Stir Fry with Noodles

Prep Time: 15 mins
Total Time: 35 mins

Servings per Recipe: 4
Calories	445 kcal
Fat	11.4 g
Carbohydrates	60.6g
Protein	18 g
Cholesterol	33 mg
Sodium	1415 mg

Ingredients

1 large skinless, boneless chicken breast, cut in bite-sized pieces
1 pinch garlic powder, or to taste
1 pinch onion powder, or to taste
freshly ground black pepper to taste
1 (8 oz) package dried rice noodles
4 C. hot water, or as needed
3 tbsp vegetable oil, divided
4 cloves garlic, minced
1 onion, chopped

1 green bell pepper, chopped
1/2 C. white cooking wine, or to taste
1/4 C. soy sauce, or to taste
2 tbsp teriyaki sauce, or to taste
1 (6 oz) can sweet baby corn, drained
3 green onions, chopped

Directions

1. Season the chicken with garlic powder, onion powder, and black pepper.
2. Fill a large bowl with hot water. Place in it the noodles and let the soak for 12 min. Remove it from the water and slice it in half.
3. Place a large wok over medium heat. Heat 1 1/2 tbsp of oil in it.
4. Add the garlic and cook it for 1 min 30 sec.
5. Stir in the bell pepper with onion and cook them for 6 min while stirring all the time. Stir in the remaining oil.
6. Add the chicken and cook them for 8 min while stirring them often. Add the wine, soy sauce, and teriyaki sauce. Cook the stir fry for 4 min.
7. Stir in the baby corn and green onions with rice and noodles.
8. Cook them for 4 min. Serve your stir fry warm. Enjoy.

Grilled
Chicken Stir Fry Linguine

🥣 Prep Time: 5 mins
🕐 Total Time: 25 mins

Servings per Recipe: 6
Calories	559 kcal
Fat	12.7 g
Carbohydrates	66.3g
Protein	43.6 g
Cholesterol	88 mg
Sodium	335 mg

Ingredients

1 (22 oz) package Tyson(R) Grilled and Ready(R) Fully Cooked Frozen Grilled Chicken Breast Strips
2 C. sliced fresh mushrooms
2 tbsp vegetable oil
2 C. frozen sweet pepper stir-fry
2/3 C. stir-fry sauce

1 lb linguine, prepared according to package directions

Directions

1. Cook the chicken according to the instructions on the package.
2. Place a large wok or wok over medium heat. Heat the oil in it. Add the mushroom and cook it for 5 min.
3. Stir in the pepper and cook them for 3 min. Stir in the chicken with sauce and cook them for 4 min.
4. Serve your stir fry hot with the linguine.
5. Enjoy.

TANGERINE
Chicken Stir Fry

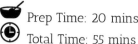 Prep Time: 20 mins
Total Time: 55 mins

Servings per Recipe: 6
Calories	467 kcal
Fat	29.2 g
Carbohydrates	17.1g
Protein	34.8 g
Cholesterol	108 mg
Sodium	552 mg

Ingredients

1/2 onion, minced
1/2 C. water
1/2 C. tangerine juice
1/3 C. coconut aminos
1/3 C. coconut oil
4 green onions, sliced into rounds
2 cloves garlic, minced
1 (1 inch) piece fresh ginger, minced
1 tsp vinegar
salt and ground black pepper to taste
2 lb boneless chicken breast, cut into cubes

1 C. string beans, trimmed, or to taste
1 C. chopped broccoli
1/4 C. ghee
1 (8 oz) package fresh mushrooms, sliced
1/2 onion, sliced
2 tbsp coconut oil
3 zucchini, spiralized
2 carrots, shredded

Directions

1. Get a mixing bowl: Mix in it the onion, water, tangerine juice, coconut aminos, 1/3 C. coconut oil, green onions, garlic, ginger, vinegar, salt, and black pepper to make the marinade.
2. Get a large mixing bowl: Toss in it half of the marinade with chicken.
3. Fill a large pot with water and a pinch of salt. Cook it until it starts boiling. Cook in it the string beans and broccoli for 2 min.
4. Remove them from the hot water and place them in a ice bath right away to cool down. Remove them from the water and place them aside.
5. Place a large wok or wok over medium heat. Melt the ghee in it. Add the mushroom and cook it for 8 min. Drain it and add it to the broccoli and bean mix.
6. Add the onion into the same wok and cook it for 8 min. Drain it and add it to the broccoli mix.
7. Drain the chicken and reserve the marinade.

8. Place a large wok over medium heat and grease it with some oil. Cook in it the chicken for 12 min while stirring them often.

9. Transfer the cooked chicken to the broccoli mix.

10. Place a large wok over medium heat. Heat 2 tbsp of coconut oil in it. Cook in it the carrot with zucchini for 4 min.

11. Stir in the remaining half of the marinade with the reserved chicken marinade and the broccoli mix. Cook them for 8 min while stirring them often.

12. Serve your stir fry chicken warm.

13. Enjoy.

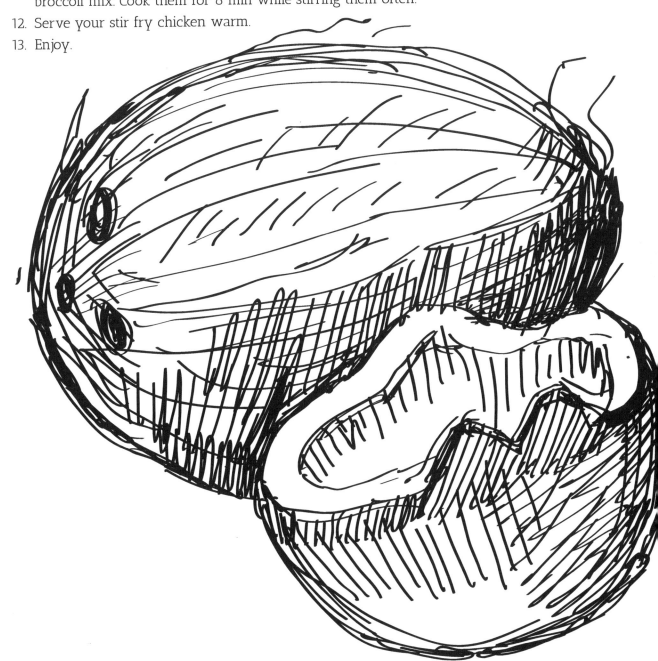

BASMATI
Chicken Stir Fry Spears

 Prep Time: 20 mins
Total Time: 1 hr 10 mins

Servings per Recipe: 4
Calories	1095 kcal
Fat	47.7 g
Carbohydrates	86.7g
Protein	77.8 g
Cholesterol	270 mg
Sodium	610 mg

Ingredients

2 C. basmati rice
4 C. water
1 tbsp vegetable oil
1 red onion, cut into 1/2-inch slices
3 1/2 lb skinless, boneless chicken thighs, cut into 2-inch strips
1 tbsp minced fresh ginger root
6 cloves garlic, minced
3 C. crimini mushrooms, cut in half
12 fresh asparagus, trimmed and cut into 2-inch pieces

2 small red bell peppers, cut into 1/2-inch strips
1 tbsp fish sauce
1 egg
2 C. fresh basil leaves
1 C. fresh cilantro leaves, chopped
2 tbsp sesame seeds, for garnish
tamari soy sauce to taste

Directions

1. Cook the rice according to the directions on the package.
2. Place a large wok or wok over medium heat. Heat the oil in it. Add the onion and cook it for 4 min.
3. Stir in the chicken with ginger and garlic. Cook them for 8 min. Stir in the mushrooms, asparagus, bell peppers, and fish sauce. Cook them for 7 min.
4. Stir in the basil and cook them for 1 min. Serve your stir fry right away with the white rice.
5. Enjoy.

Beachy
Chicken Stir Fry

🥣 Prep Time: 20 mins
🕐 Total Time: 42 mins

Servings per Recipe: 4
Calories	419 kcal
Fat	12.5 g
Carbohydrates	49.1g
Protein	30.4 g
Cholesterol	61 mg
Sodium	579 mg

Ingredients

14 oz skinless, boneless chicken breast, thinly sliced
1 egg white, beaten
2 tsp cornstarch
1 tsp sesame oil
1 (8 oz) package Chinese egg noodles
2 tbsp vegetable oil, or as needed
1/2 C. chicken broth
3 spring onions, chopped, or to taste
1 1/2 tbsp light soy sauce
1 tbsp rice wine (sake)

1/2 tsp ground white pepper
1/2 tsp ground black pepper
1 tbsp cornstarch
2 tsp water
2 tbsp oyster sauce
1 C. fresh bean sprouts, or to taste

Directions

1. Cook the noodles according to the instructions on the package. Place it aside. Get a large mixing bowl: Mix in it the chicken with egg white, 2 tsp cornstarch, and sesame oil.

2. Place a large wok over medium heat. Heat the oil in it. Cook in it the noodles until it becomes golden and slightly crisp for 4 min on each side. Remove it from the wok and place it aside.

3. Add the chicken to the wok and cook it for 4 min. Drain and it and place it aside. Stir the stock with spring onions, soy sauce, rice wine, white pepper, and black pepper into the same wok.

4. Get a small mixing bowl: Whisk in it 1 tbsp cornstarch and water. Add the mix to the wok with oyster sauce, chicken and bean sprouts.

5. Cook them until the mix becomes thick. Serve your stir fry with the noodles warm. Enjoy.

FRIED
Teriyaki Chicken Rice

 Prep Time: 15 mins
Total Time: 23 mins

Servings per Recipe: 4
Calories	506 kcal
Fat	16.5 g
Carbohydrates	55.3g
Protein	32 g
Cholesterol	65 mg
Sodium	800 mg

Ingredients

1 lb skinless, boneless chicken breasts,
cut into thin strips
1/4 C. teriyaki sauce, divided
3 tbsp vegetable oil, divided
3 scallions, thinly sliced
2 cloves garlic, minced
1 tbsp minced fresh ginger root

8 oz snow peas, trimmed
1/4 C. low-sodium chicken broth
4 C. cooked white rice
3 tbsp chopped roasted cashews

Directions

1. Get a large mixing bowl: Toss in it the chicken and 2 tbsp teriyaki sauce.
2. Place a large wok over medium heat. Heat 1 1/2 tbsp of oil in it. Cook in it the chicken for 6 min. Drain and place it aside.
3. Add the scallions, garlic, ginger, and remaining vegetable oil to the same pan. Cook them for 2 min. Add the broth with snow peas. Cook them for 4 min.
4. Add the rice, cooked chicken, and remaining teriyaki sauce. Cook them for 4 min. Fold in the cashews. Serve your stir fry warm.
5. Enjoy.

American
Parsley Chicken Stir Fry

🥣 Prep Time: 10 mins

🕐 Total Time: 40 mins

Servings per Recipe: 1	
Calories	425 kcal
Fat	9.4 g
Carbohydrates	61.2g
Protein	21.2 g
Cholesterol	44 mg
Sodium	786 mg

Ingredients

2 C. uncooked white rice

4 C. water

1 tbsp olive oil

1 tsp garlic salt

1 tsp black pepper

1 tsp dried parsley

3 skinless, boneless chicken breast halves, cut into strips

2 C. chopped broccoli

1 C. sliced carrots

1 C. sugar snap peas

1 (10.75 oz) can condensed cheddar cheese soup, such as Campbell's(R)

1/2 C. shredded Cheddar cheese

Directions

1. Cook the rice according to the directions on the package.
2. Place a large wok over medium heat. Heat the oil in it. Add the garlic salt, black pepper, chicken and parsley. Cook them for 8 min.
3. Add the broccoli, carrots, and snap peas. Put on the lid and cook them for 7 min.
4. Add the condensed Cheddar cheese soup. Stir them well. Cook them until they start simmering while stirring them often.
5. Serve your stir fry hot with rice.
6. Enjoy.

CREAMY
Canola Chicken Stir Fry

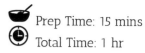

Prep Time: 15 mins
Total Time: 1 hr

Servings per Recipe: 6

Calories	299 kcal
Fat	17.4 g
Carbohydrates	14.8g
Protein	21.2 g
Cholesterol	64 mg
Sodium	1341 mg

Ingredients

1/4 C. water
3 tbsp light soy sauce
2 tbsp canola oil
2 tbsp cornstarch
1 tbsp sesame oil
1 1/2 tsp white sugar
3/4 tsp salt
1/2 tsp garlic powder
1 (20 oz) package skinless, boneless chicken thighs, sliced

1 head cauliflower, cut into florets
1/4 C. canola oil for frying, or as needed
4 cloves garlic, smashed
1 C. water, or to taste, divided
1 (10.75 oz) can cream of mushroom soup (such as Campbell's(R))
1/4 C. oyster sauce
3/4 tsp white sugar
3/4 tsp salt

Directions

1. Get a large mixing bowl: Whisk in it 1/4 C. water, soy sauce, 2 tbsp canola oil, cornstarch, sesame oil, 1 1/2 tsp sugar, 3/4 tsp salt, and garlic powder.

2. Add the chicken and coat it with the marinade. Wrap a plastic foil on the bowl and place it in the fridge for 40 min to an overnight.

3. Fill a large pot of water. Cook it until it starts boiling. Cook in it the cauliflower for 6 min. Remove it from the water and place it in an ice bath right away.

4. Allow it lose heat completely fro few minutes. Drain it and place it aside. Place a large wok over medium heat. Heat the oil in it. Cook in it the garlic with a pinch of salt for 2 min 30 sec while pressing it with the back of the spatula.

5. Drain the garlic and discard it. Remove the chicken from the marinade and discard it. Add it to the hot wok and cook it for 6 min. Add 1/2 C. of water and scrap the bottom of the pan.

6. Stir in the cream of mushroom soup and remaining 1/2 C. water, oyster sauce, 3/4 tsp sugar, cauliflower, and 3/4 tsp salt. Cook them for 8 min until the sauce becomes thick. Serve your stir fry hot. Enjoy.

Chipotle
Chicken Stir Fry

Prep Time: 20 mins
Total Time: 35 mins

Servings per Recipe: 4
Calories	427 kcal
Fat	26 g
Carbohydrates	14.6g
Protein	29.9 g
Cholesterol	96 mg
Sodium	653 mg

Ingredients

1 1/2 lb boneless chicken thighs, cut into bite-size pieces
2 tbsp chipotle chile-flavored olive oil
2 tbsp soy sauce
1/2 tsp red pepper flakes
1 tbsp garlic-flavored olive oil, or more as needed
1 C. sugar snap peas
1 C. chopped onion
1/2 C. chopped red bell pepper

1/2 C. chopped orange bell pepper
1 tbsp minced garlic
1/4 C. white wine
1 tsp garlic pepper seasoning
1/2 tsp ground ginger
1 tbsp cornstarch
1 tbsp water, or as needed
1 C. sliced fresh mushrooms

Directions

1. Get a small mixing bowl: Whisk in it the chicken, chipotle-flavored olive oil, soy sauce, and red pepper flakes.
2. Place a large wok over medium heat. Heat the garlic flavored oil. Sauté in it the snap peas, onion, red bell pepper, orange bell pepper, and garlic for 7 min.
3. Stir in the white wine, garlic pepper seasoning, and ground ginger. Cook them for 6 min.
4. Get a small mixing bowl: Mix in it the cornstarch with water. Stir the mix into the wok with mushroom. Cook them for 6 min until the sauce becomes thick.
5. Serve your stir fry hot with some white rice.
6. Enjoy.

CASHEW
Chicken Breasts Stir Fry

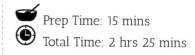

Prep Time: 15 mins
Total Time: 2 hrs 25 mins

Servings per Recipe: 4

Calories	501 kcal
Fat	24.6 g
Carbohydrates	38g
Protein	36.9 g
Cholesterol	66 mg
Sodium	783 mg

Ingredients

2 (8 oz) skinless, boneless chicken breast halves, cut into thin strips
3 tbsp light soy sauce
1 (2 inch) piece fresh ginger, peeled and finely chopped
1 tbsp chopped fresh tarragon
1 tbsp brown sugar
salt and ground black pepper to taste
1 tbsp vegetable oil
1 C. unsalted cashews

2 large carrots, peeled and cut into matchstick-size pieces
1 head cabbage, sliced
1 C. baby kale
1 tbsp sesame oil

Directions

1. Get a large mixing bowl: Whisk in it the soy sauce, ginger, tarragon, and brown sugar. Add the chicken and stir them to coat.
2. Place a piece of plastic on the bowl to cover it. Place it in the fridge for 3 h.
3. Place a large wok or wok over medium heat. Heat the oil in it. Remove the chicken from the marinade it add it to the pan. Cook it for 6 min.
4. Stir in the chicken marinade. Cook them until they start boiling for 4 min. Add the carrots with cashews. Cook them for 2 min.
5. Divide the cabbage and kale on 4 serving plates then drizzle the sesame oil over them. Top them with the chicken stir fry. Serve them right away.
6. Enjoy.

Teriyaki Chicken Tortellini Stir Fry

🥣 Prep Time: 30 mins
🕐 Total Time: 50 mins

Servings per Recipe: 4
Calories	455 kcal
Fat	21.4 g
Carbohydrates	40.1g
Protein	24.9 g
Cholesterol	88 mg
Sodium	719 mg

Ingredients

1/4 lb refrigerated cheese tortellini
1 tbsp sesame oil
1 (12 oz) package teriyaki ginger chicken meatballs
1/2 C. pineapple chunks, drained
1 tbsp hoisin sauce
2 tbsp extra-virgin olive oil
1 C. chopped broccoli florets
1 C. chopped cauliflower florets
2 carrots, chopped

1/2 green bell pepper, chopped
1/2 red bell pepper, chopped
1/2 small zucchini, peeled and sliced
1/2 C. chopped celery
4 green onions, chopped
1/8 tsp sea salt
1/8 tsp ground black pepper
1 tbsp chopped fresh parsley (optional)
1 tbsp grated Parmesan cheese (optional)

Directions

1. Cook the tortellini according to the directions on the package.
2. Place a large wok over medium heat. Heat the oil in it. Cook in it the meatballs, pineapple chunks, and hoisin sauce for 9 min.
3. Drain the mix and place them aside. Place another wok over medium heat. Heat the oil in it. Cook in it the broccoli, cauliflower, carrots, green bell pepper, red bell pepper, zucchini, celery, and green onions with a pinch of salt and pepper.
4. Cook them for 7 min. Fold in the cooked meatballs mix with tortellini and cook them the for 2 min. Serve your stir fry hot.
5. Enjoy.

SUMMER
Chicken Stir Fry

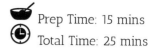 Prep Time: 15 mins
Total Time: 25 mins

Servings per Recipe: 4	
Calories	164 kcal
Fat	8.2 g
Carbohydrates	15.2g
Protein	9.7 g
Cholesterol	21 mg
Sodium	95 mg

Ingredients

1 tbsp olive oil
1 small onion, chopped
1 red bell pepper, chopped
2 ears corn, kernels cut from cob
1 large zucchini, chopped
1/2 C. chopped cooked chicken
1/4 C. chopped fresh parsley

1/4 C. shredded Colby-Monterey Jack cheese, divided
salt and ground black pepper to taste

Directions

1. Place a large wok over medium heat. Heat the oil in it. Cook in it the red pepper with onion for 4 min.
2. Add the corn, zucchini, and chicken. Cook them for 7 min while stirring often.
3. Top the chicken stir fry with half of the cheese and all the parsley, a pinch of salt and pepper. Stir them and cook them for 2 min until the cheese melts.
4. Serve your stir fry hot with the remaining cheese on top.
5. Enjoy.

Roasted
Nutty Chicken Stir Fry

🥣 Prep Time: 10 mins

🕐 Total Time: 35 mins

Servings per Recipe: 6

Calories	437 kcal
Fat	29.1 g
Carbohydrates	18.8g
Protein	29.7 g
Cholesterol	46 mg
Sodium	155 mg

Ingredients

1 tbsp wok oil or peanut oil
1 lb skinless, boneless chicken breast halves - cut into bite-size pieces
1 medium red bell pepper, chopped
1 1/2 C. chicken broth
2 tsp soy sauce
1 tbsp sugar
1 clove garlic, minced
1 (1 inch) piece fresh ginger root, peeled and chopped

1/4 tsp ground cayenne pepper
1 tbsp cornstarch
1 bunch green onions, chopped
1 bunch cilantro, chopped
2 C. chopped dry roasted peanuts

Directions

1. Place a large wok over medium heat. Heat the oil in it. Cook in it the chicken for 6 min. Add the bell pepper and cook them until they become tender.
2. Get a small mixing bowl: Whisk in it the broth, soy sauce, sugar, garlic, cayenne pepper, ginger, and cornstarch. Stir it into the wok with green onion and cilantro.
3. Cook them for 6 min until the sauce becomes thick. Fold in it the roasted peanuts. Serve your stir fry hot.
4. Enjoy.

SPICY
Chicken Noodles Stir Fry

Prep Time: 20 mins
Total Time: 35 mins

Servings per Recipe: 4
Calories	503 kcal
Fat	16.5 g
Carbohydrates	69.8g
Protein	26.5 g
Cholesterol	29 mg
Sodium	3868 mg

Ingredients

2 tbsp canola oil
1 tbsp sesame oil
2 skinless, boneless chicken breast
halves - cut into bite-size pieces
2 cloves garlic, minced
2 tbsp Asian-style chile paste
1/2 C. soy sauce
1 tbsp canola oil
1/2 medium head cabbage, thinly sliced
1 onion, sliced

2 carrots, cut into matchsticks
1 tbsp salt
2 lb cooked yakisoba noodles
2 tbsp pickled ginger, or to taste
(optional)

Directions

1. Place a large wok over medium heat. Heat 2 tbsp of canola oil and sesame oil in it. Cook in it the garlic with chicken for 2 min..
2. Add chili paste and cook them for 5 min. Stir in the soy sauce and cook them for 3 min. Transfer the chicken mix into a bowl and place it aside.
3. Heat 1 tbsp of canola oil in the same pan. Cook in it the cabbage, onion, carrots, and salt for 5 min.
4. Add back the chicken mix with noodles. Cook them for 5 min. Serve your stir fry hot.
5. Enjoy.

Spicy Chestnut Chicken Stir Fry

Prep Time: 30 mins
Total Time: 1 hr 30 mins

Servings per Recipe: 4
Calories	437 kcal
Fat	23.3 g
Carbohydrates	25.3g
Protein	34.4 g
Cholesterol	66 mg
Sodium	596 mg

Ingredients

1 lb skinless, boneless chicken breast halves - cut into chunks
2 tbsp white wine
2 tbsp soy sauce
2 tbsp sesame oil, divided
2 tbsp cornstarch, dissolved in 2 tbsp water
1 oz hot chile paste
1 tsp distilled white vinegar
2 tsp brown sugar

4 green onions, chopped
1 tbsp chopped garlic
1 (8 oz) can water chestnuts
4 oz chopped peanuts

Directions

1. Get a large mixing bowl: Whisk in it 1 tbsp wine, 1 tbsp soy sauce, 1 tbsp oil, 1 tbsp cornstarch and water mix. Mix them well.

2. Add the chicken and stir them well. Place the mix in the fridge for 40 min.

3. Get a small mixing bowl: Stir in it 1 tbsp wine, 1 tbsp soy sauce, 1 tbsp oil, 1 tbsp cornstarch and water mix, chili paste, vinegar and sugar.

4. Stir in the green onion, garlic, water chestnuts and peanuts to make the sauce.

5. Place a large wok over medium heat. Cook in it the sauce for 2 min.

6. Place a another wok over medium heat. Grease it with some oil. Drain the chicken and cook it in the wok for 6 min.

7. Stir in the sauce into the chicken and cook them until the sauce becomes slightly thick. Serve your chicken stir fry warm.

8. Enjoy.

CARROT, Cabbage, and Chicken Wok

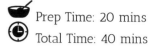

Prep Time: 20 mins
Total Time: 40 mins

Servings per Recipe: 6	
Calories	369 kcal
Fat	4.9 g
Carbohydrates	65.1g
Protein	18.1 g
Cholesterol	35 mg
Sodium	789 mg

Ingredients

1 (12 oz) package dried rice noodles
1 tsp vegetable oil
1 onion, finely diced
3 cloves garlic, minced
2 C. diced cooked chicken breast meat
1 small head cabbage, thinly sliced

4 carrot, thinly sliced
1/4 C. soy sauce
2 lemons - cut into wedges, for garnish

Directions

1. Get a large bowl: Fill it with hot water. Place it in the noodles and place it aside until it becomes soft.
2. Place a large wok over medium heat. Heat the oil in it. Add the garlic with onion and cook them for 3 min.
3. Stir in the carrot with chicken and cabbage. Cook them for 6 min. Stir in the noodles and cook them for 3 min while stirring constantly. Serve your chicken stir fry hot.
4. Enjoy.

Sweet and Salty Chicken Stir Fry

Prep Time: 20 mins
Total Time: 40 mins

Servings per Recipe: 4
Calories   615 kcal
Fat   33.2 g
Carbohydrates   37.9g
Protein   43 g
Cholesterol   129 mg
Sodium   1967 mg

Ingredients

3/4 C. dark brown sugar
1/3 C. cold water
1/3 C. fish sauce
1/3 C. rice vinegar
1 tbsp soy sauce
4 cloves garlic, crushed
1 tbsp fresh grated ginger
1 tsp vegetable oil
8 boneless, skinless chicken thighs, quartered

1/2 C. roasted peanuts
2 fresh jalapeno peppers, seeded and sliced
1 bunch green onions, chopped
fresh cilantro sprigs, for garnish

Directions

1. Get a medium mixing bowl: Combine in it the brown sugar, water, fish sauce, rice vinegar, soy sauce, garlic, and ginger. Mix them well to make the sauce and place it aside for 2 min.
2. Place a large wok over medium heat. Heat the oil in it. Cook in it the chicken with 1/3 C. of the sauce for 8 min.
3. Stir in the remaining sauce and cook them for 7 min. Add the peanuts, jalapenos and green onion. Cook them for 4 min.
4. Serve your chicken stir fry hot with some rice.
5. Enjoy.

CHILI
Fried Chicken Breast Bites

Prep Time: 30 mins
Total Time: 50 mins

Servings per Recipe: 4
Calories	740 kcal
Fat	37 g
Carbohydrates	68.3g
Protein	34 g
Cholesterol	86 mg
Sodium	1113 mg

Ingredients

2 tbsp soy sauce
1 tbsp dry sherry
1 dash sesame oil
2 tbsp all-purpose flour
2 tbsp cornstarch
2 tbsp water
1/4 tsp baking powder
1/4 tsp baking soda
1 tsp canola oil
4 (5 oz) skinless, boneless chicken breast halves, cut into 1-inch cubes
1 quart vegetable oil for frying

1/2 C. water
1 C. chicken broth
1/4 C. distilled white vinegar
1/4 C. cornstarch
1 C. white sugar
2 tbsp soy sauce
2 tbsp sesame oil
1 tsp red chile paste (such as Thai Kitchen(R))
1 clove garlic, minced
2 tbsp toasted sesame seeds

Directions

1. Get a large mixing bowl: Mix in it the 2 tbsp soy sauce, the dry sherry, dash of sesame oil, flour, 2 tbsp cornstarch, 2 tbsp water, baking powder, baking soda, and canola oil. Add the chicken and stir them.

2. Place a plastic wrap over the bowl. Place it in the fridge for 30 min. Heat the oil in a heavy saucepan until it reaches 375 F. Place a heavy saucepan over medium heat:

3. Stir in it 1/2 C. water, chicken broth, vinegar, 1/4 C. cornstarch, sugar, 2 tbsp soy sauce, 2 tbsp sesame oil, red chili paste, and garlic . Cook them until they start boiling while stirring all the time to make the sauce.

4. Lower the heat and keep cooking the sauce until it becomes slightly thick. Drain the chicken from the marinade and deep fry it for 4 to 6 min or until it becomes golden brown.

5. Remove the chicken dices from the hot oil and serve them with the sauce warm. Enjoy.

Wild
Hoisin Chicken Stir Fry

Prep Time: 20 mins
Total Time: 30 mins

Servings per Recipe: 2
Calories   635 kcal
Fat   30 g
Carbohydrates   56.6g
Protein   37.1 g
Cholesterol   69 mg
Sodium   473 mg

Ingredients

1 whole boneless, skinless chicken breast, cubed
2 C. wild rice, cooked
1/2 lb fresh asparagus
3 tbsp hoisin sauce

4 tbsp peanut oil
1 tbsp brown sugar

Directions

1. Slice the asparagus spears into 3/4 inch pieces.
2. Get a small mixing bowl: Whisk in it the brown sugar with hoisin sauce to make the sauce.
3. Place a large wok over medium heat. Heat 1 tbsp of oil in it. Cook in it the asparagus for 3 min. Drain it and place it aside.
4. Heat the rest of oil in the same wok. Cook in it the chicken for 6 to 8 min. Add back the asparagus with the sauce. Cook them for 2 min.
5. Serve your chicken stir fry with rice.
6. Enjoy.

PLUM
Peanut and Chicken Stir Fry

 Prep Time: 15 mins
Total Time: 35 mins

Servings per Recipe: 2

Calories	549 kcal
Fat	21.4 g
Carbohydrates	41g
Protein	44.3 g
Cholesterol	104 mg
Sodium	1621 mg

Ingredients

1 tbsp vegetable oil
1 green bell pepper, seeded and cubed
1 red bell pepper, seeded and cubed
1/4 C. sliced sweet onions
3/4 lb skinless, boneless chicken breast,
cut into strips
2 1/2 tsp Caribbean jerk seasoning

1/2 C. plum sauce
1 tbsp soy sauce
1/4 C. chopped roasted peanuts

Directions

1. Place a large wok or wok over medium heat. Heat the oil in it. Add the onion with pepper and cook them for 8 min. Drain the mix and place it aside.
2. Stir in the chicken with jerk seasoning. Cook it for 6 min. Add the plum sauce with onion and pepper mix. Stir them well. Cook them for 6 min.
3. Fold in the soy sauce with peanuts. Serve your stir fry warm.
4. Enjoy.

Beginners' Creamy Chicken Stir Fry

Prep Time: 20 mins

Total Time: 1 hr 20 mins

Servings per Recipe: 4

Calories	305 kcal
Fat	17.5 g
Carbohydrates	8.3g
Protein	28.1 g
Cholesterol	96 mg
Sodium	1102 mg

Ingredients

1 lb skinless, boneless chicken breast halves, cut into bite size pieces
1/2 onion, chopped
1 green bell pepper, chopped
1/4 C. butter
1 tsp paprika
1 tsp garlic salt
seasoning salt to taste
1 (10.75 oz) can condensed cream of mushroom soup
1/2 C. water

Directions

1. Place a large wok or wok over low heat. Heat the butter in it until it melts. Add the chicken, onion and green bell pepper then cook them for 7 min.
2. Add the paprika garlic salt and seasoned salt. Put on the lid and cook them for 17 min. Stir in the water with soup and bring them to a simmer.
3. Cook the stir fry until it becomes thick. Serve it hot with some rice.
4. Enjoy.

Beginners' Creamy Chicken Stir Fry

ITALIAN
Bell Chicken Stir Fry

 Prep Time: 15 mins
Total Time: 30 mins

Servings per Recipe: 4

Calories	210 kcal
Fat	7.9 g
Carbohydrates	10.2g
Protein	24.2 g
Cholesterol	59 mg
Sodium	297 mg

Ingredients

2 tbsp all-purpose flour
1 tsp garlic powder
salt and pepper to taste
1 lb skinless, boneless chicken breast
meat - cut into cubes
1 tsp vegetable oil
1 red bell pepper, sliced

1 small onion, chopped
1 C. sliced zucchini
1 C. sliced fresh mushrooms
1/4 C. chicken broth
1/4 C. Italian salad dressing

Directions

1. Get a zip lock bag: Combine in it the flour, garlic powder, salt, and pepper with chicken dices. Seal the bag and toss them to coat.
2. Place a large wok or wok over medium heat. Heat the oil in it. Cook in it the chicken dices for 7 min.
3. Add the bell pepper, onion, zucchini, mushrooms, chicken broth, and Italian dressing. Put on the lid and cook them for 12 min. Serve your stir fry hot with rice or noodles.
4. Enjoy.

Oriental
Chili Chicken and Ramen Stir Fry

Prep Time: 15 mins
Total Time: 30 mins

Servings per Recipe: 2

Calories	438 kcal
Fat	14.1 g
Carbohydrates	47.6g
Protein	31.9 g
Cholesterol	65 mg
Sodium	1118 mg

Ingredients

1 1/2 C. hot water
1 (3 oz) package Oriental-flavor ramen noodle soup mix
2 tsp vegetable oil, divided
8 oz skinless, boneless chicken breast halves, cut into 2-inch strips
2 C. broccoli florets
1 C. sliced onion wedges
2 cloves garlic, minced

1 C. fresh bean sprouts
1/2 C. water
1/2 C. sliced water chestnuts
1 tsp soy sauce
1 tsp oyster sauce
1/4 tsp chile-garlic sauce (such as Sriracha(R)), or to taste
1 roma tomato, cut into wedges

Directions

1. Pour 1 1/2 C. of water in a heavy saucepan. Cook in it the noodles for 3 min. Remove it from the water and place it aside.
2. Place a large wok or wok over medium heat. Heat 1 tsp of oil in it. Add the chicken and cook it for 7 min. Drain the chicken and place it aside.
3. Turn the heat to high. Add the broccoli, onion, and garlic. Cook them for 7 min.
4. Stir in the ramen seasoning packet with noodles, bean sprouts, water, water chestnuts, soy sauce, oyster sauce, and chile-garlic sauce.
5. Cook them for 6 min. Stir in the tomato and cook them for 4 min. Serve your stir fry hot.
6. Enjoy.

CORNY
Grilled Chicken Stir Fry

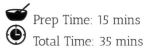

Prep Time: 15 mins
Total Time: 35 mins

Servings per Recipe: 4

Calories	313 kcal
Fat	9.6 g
Carbohydrates	29.1g
Protein	25 g
Cholesterol	52 mg
Sodium	915 mg

Ingredients

3 skinless, boneless chicken breast halves - cut into strips
2 tbsp olive oil
1 onion, sliced
1 red bell pepper, seeded and cubed
1 yellow bell pepper, seeded and cubed
1 (15 oz) can baby corn, drained

1 tbsp white sugar
1 (16 oz) package frozen stir-fry vegetables
1 C. water
1 tbsp cornstarch
1 tbsp soy sauce

Directions

1. Before you do anything preheat the grill and grease it.
2. Cook the chicken strips in the grill for 8 min. Place them aside to lose heat completely. Cut them into dices.
3. Place a large wok or wok over medium heat. Heat the oil in it. Cook in it the onion for 3 min.
4. Stir in the red and yellow pepper, baby corn, and the stir-fry veggies. Turn the heat to high medium. Cook them for 17 min.
5. Get a small mixing bowl: Whisk in it the cornstarch with water.
6. Stir in the salt with chicken, sugar, soy sauce, and cornstarch mix. Cook them until the stir fry becomes thick. Serve it hot with some rice or noodles.
7. Enjoy.

Peanut Butter
Chicken Stir Fry

Prep Time: 15 mins
Total Time: 30 mins

Servings per Recipe: 4
Calories	344 kcal
Fat	16.6 g
Carbohydrates	24.4g
Protein	28 g
Cholesterol	54 mg
Sodium	412 mg

Ingredients

1/2 C. chicken broth
2 C. sliced mushrooms
1/2 sweet onion, sliced
1 small head broccoli, cut into spears
1 tbsp tamari or soy sauce
1/4 C. creamy peanut butter
1 pinch red pepper flakes (optional)
1 (12 oz) package shredded coleslaw mix
3 C. bean sprouts

1 (9 oz) package diced cooked chicken breast meat
1 tbsp toasted sesame seeds (optional)

Directions

1. Place a large wok over medium heat. Pour the broth in it. Cook it until it starts boiling.
2. Stir in the broccoli with onion and mushroom. Put on the lid and cook them for 6 min. Add the tamari, peanut butter, and pepper flakes. Mix them until they become smooth.
3. Stir in the coleslaw mix, bean sprouts, and chicken. Cook them for 4 min. Serve your stir fry hot.
4. Enjoy.

A TEXAS-MEXICAN
Stir Fry

🍳 Prep Time: 20 mins
🕐 Total Time: 35 mins

Servings per Recipe: 4
Calories	333 kcal
Carbohydrates	13.3 g
Cholesterol	94 mg
Fat	5.9 g
Protein	32.1 g
Sodium	945 mg

Ingredients

1 tsp olive oil
1 green bell pepper, chopped
1 red bell pepper, chopped
2 tbsps all-purpose flour, or as needed
1 (1 ounce) packet taco seasoning mix
1 pound skinless, boneless chicken
breast halves, diced

2 tsps olive oil
1 (15 ounce) can black beans, rinsed and
drained
1/2 cup prepared salsa
1 cup shredded Cheddar cheese

Directions

1. Get a wok, heat 1 tsp olive oil. Fry red and green peppers for 5 mins, remove them.
2. Grab a bowl combine the following: taco seasoning and flour. Add your chicken. Coat the chicken.
3. Get your wok. Heat 2 tsps of olive oil. Fry chicken for five mins, until cooked.
4. Combine the peppers from earlier with the chicken and also add some salsa, and black beans.
5. Stir fry, the chicken, the peppers, the beans, and salsa for 5 mins.
6. Serve with cheddar cheese.
7. Enjoy.

Grapes
and Chicken Wok

Prep Time: 15 mins
Total Time: 25 mins

Servings per Recipe: 4
Calories	226 kcal
Fat	6.5 g
Carbohydrates	29.4g
Protein	12 g
Cholesterol	26 mg
Sodium	23 mg

Ingredients

1 tbsp vegetable oil
1 C. sliced red grapes
1 C. cubed cooked chicken

2 C. cooked rice
1/4 C. chicken broth

Directions

1. Stir fry your chicken and grapes in hot veggie oil for 4 mins.
2. Now add the broth and rice.
3. Let the contents cook for 4 more mins until everything is hot.
4. Enjoy.

TOFU
and Miso
(豆腐みそ)

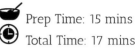

Prep Time: 15 mins
Total Time: 17 mins

Servings per Recipe: 6
Calories   82 kcal
Carbohydrates   4.6 g
Cholesterol   6 mg
Fat   4.5 g
Protein   7.4 g
Sodium   358 mg

Ingredients

2 tbsps sesame seeds
1/2 cup dried Asian-style whole sardines
2 1/2 tbsps red miso paste
1/2 cup boiling water

1 (16 ounce) package silken tofu, cubed
4 green onions, thinly sliced
crushed red pepper flakes

Directions

1. Get a wok and fry sesame seeds until aromatic for 3 mins.
2. Get a wok and begin to boil water.
3. Get a food processor and combine dried sardines and sesame seeds. Process into a powder.
4. Put sesame and sardines in a bowl and combine miso. Combine in your boiling water (1/2 cup) from earlier and mix until creamy.
5. Finally combine your tofu red pepper, and green onions.
6. Enjoy.

Teriyaki
Chicken Rice Stir Fry

Prep Time: 20 mins
Total Time: 40 mins

Servings per Recipe: 6

Calories	246 kcal
Fat	6.5 g
Carbohydrates	33.8g
Protein	12 g
Cholesterol	51 mg
Sodium	803 mg

Ingredients

1/2 lb boneless skinless chicken breasts
2 tbsp vegetable oil
3 green onions and tops, chopped
1 carrot, julienned
1 egg, beaten

4 C. cold cooked rice
3 tbsp teriyaki sauce

Directions

1. Slice the chicken breasts into thin strips.
2. Place a large wok over medium heat. Heat the oil in it. Cook in it the carrot with onion and chicken for 4 min.
3. Stir in the egg and cook them for 2 min. Add the rice and cook them for 4 min while stirring often.
4. Stir in the teriyaki sauce. Turn off the heat and serve your stir fry right away.
5. Enjoy

TILAPIA FILLETS
with Teriyaki Sauce

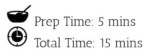

Prep Time: 5 mins
Total Time: 15 mins

Servings per Recipe: 5
Calories	245.6
Fat	4.8g
Cholesterol	62.5mg
Sodium	1680.0mg
Carbohydrates	23.3g
Protein	28.1g

Ingredients

1 tbsp oil
5 tilapia fillets
1/2 C. brown sugar
1/4 C. seasoned rice wine vinegar
1/2 C. soy sauce

1 tsp fresh ginger, grated
1/2 tsp garlic, minced

Directions

1. Place a large wok over medium heat. Add the oil and heat it. Lay in it the tilapia Fillets.
2. Get a mixing bowl: Mix in it the remaining ingredients to make the sauce. Pour the sauce all over the tilapia. Cook them until the fish is done and sauce is thick.
3. Serve your tilapia fillets with teriyaki sauce warm.
4. Enjoy.

Glazed
Salmon Fillets with Orzo

Prep Time: 15 mins
Total Time: 25 mins

Servings per Recipe: 4
Calories   849.7
Fat   31.3g
Cholesterol   153.6mg
Sodium   3001.4mg
Carbohydrates   55.8g
Protein   81.8g

Ingredients

4 salmon fillets (2 lbs
1 oz. canola oil
1 oz. soy sauce
8 oz. teriyaki sauce
8 oz. orzo pasta, precooked
2 garlic cloves, minced
2 tbsp olive oil, combined with garlic

1/2 C. red bell pepper, diced
1/3 C. parmesan cheese
8 oz. spinach, julienned

Directions

1. Before you do anything preheat the grill and grease it.
2. Coat the salmon fillets with soy sauce and brush them with the oil. Cook them in the grill for 4 min on each side.
3. Brush the salmon fillets with 2 oz. of teriyaki glaze. Cook them for 3 min on each side.
4. Cook the orzo according to the directions on the package.
5. Place a large wok over medium heat. Heat the oil in it. Add the garlic with peppers and orzo. Cook them for 2 min.
6. Stir in the cheese until it melts. Turn off the heat and add the spinach. Stir them several times until the spinach wilts.
7. Serve your orzo with the glazed salmon fillets and the remaining teriyaki sauce.
8. Enjoy.

TERIYAKI
Burgers

Prep Time: 30 mins
Total Time: 45 mins

Servings per Recipe: 4
Calories	402.7
Fat	11.1g
Cholesterol	93.0mg
Sodium	31740.4mg
Carbohydrates	62.8g
Protein	213.5g

Ingredients

1/2 tbsp peanut oil
1/2 C. onion (purple)
1 C. zucchini
1/2 C. red bell pepper
2 eggs
1/2 tsp ginger (ground)
1/2 tsp cumin
1/4 C. soy sauce

1/4 C. teriyaki sauce
1/4 C. walnut pieces
1 1/2 C. brown rice (cooked)

Directions

1. Before you do anything heat the oven on 350 F.
2. Chop the bell pepper with zucchini until they become fine. Mince the onion.
3. Place a large wok on medium heat. Add the oil and heat it. Stir in the onion and cook it for 6 min.
4. Stir in the chopped zucchini with bell pepper to the onion. Cook them for 16 min while stirring occasionally. Turn off the heat and allow the mix to lose heat.
5. Get a mixing bowl: Add the eggs and beat them. Stir in the onion mix with ginger, cumin, soy sauce, teriyaki sauce, walnuts and cooked rice. Mix them well. Shape the mix into 4 burgers.
6. Place the burgers on the baking pan. Cook them in the oven for 8 min on each side.
7. Assemble your burgers with your favorite toppings. Serve them right away.
8. Enjoy.

Beef Stir-Fry (牛肉の炒め)

Prep Time: 30 mins
Total Time: 45 mins

Servings per Recipe: 8

Calories	290 kcal
Carbohydrates	26.4 g
Cholesterol	39 mg
Fat	7.6 g
Protein	26.4 g
Sodium	1271 mg

Ingredients

2 pounds boneless beef sirloin or beef top round steaks (3/4" thick)
3 tbsps cornstarch
1 (10.5 ounce) can Campbell's® Condensed Beef Broth
1/2 cup soy sauce
2 tbsps sugar
2 tbsps vegetable oil

4 cups sliced shiitake mushrooms
1 head Chinese cabbage (bok choy), thinly sliced
2 medium red peppers, cut into 2"-long strips
3 stalks celery, sliced
2 medium green onions, cut into 2" pieces
Hot cooked regular long-grain white rice

Directions

1. To start this recipe grab a knife and begin to cut your beef into some thin long strips. Grab a medium sized bowl and combine the following ingredients: sugar, broth, soy, and cornstarch.
2. After combining the ingredients set them aside.
3. Get your wok hot over a high level of heat and add one 1 tbsp of oil to it.
4. Once your oil is hot combine the following ingredients in it: green onions, mushrooms, celery, cabbage, and peppers.
5. Fry these veggies down until you find that they are soft. Set aside.
6. Now grab your cornstarch mixture and put it in the pot. Stir-fry until you find that it has thickened.
7. Once thick, combine the cornstarch with your beef and veggies.
8. Fry until beef is cooked completely.
9. Let contents cool.
10. Enjoy.

RAMEN
Sesame Soup

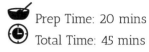 Prep Time: 20 mins
Total Time: 45 mins

Servings per Recipe: 4
Calories	467.9
Fat	21.3g
Cholesterol	78.2mg
Sodium	1630.6mg
Carbohydrates	35.4g
Protein	33.3g

Ingredients

1 lb top round steak, julienne
1 tbsp peanut oil
1/2 tbsp sesame oil
1 inch fresh ginger, finely grated
2 cloves garlic, minced
1/4-1/2 tsp crushed red pepper flakes
3 C. beef stock
2 bunches scallions, diced

2 tbsp rice wine vinegar
2 (3 oz.) packets ramen noodles, packet removed
1/2 C. baby carrots, grated

Directions

1. Place a large wok over medium heat. Heat in it 1/3 of each of the oils.
2. Sauté in it the ginger, garlic and red chilies. Cook them for 1 min. Stir in 1/3 of the beef slices. Cook them for 4 min. Place the mix aside.
3. Repeat the process with the remaining beef and oil until it is done.
4. Place a large saucepan over medium heat. Stir in it the Stock, Vinegar,& Scallions. Cook them until they start boiling.
5. Lower the heat and cook it until it starts boiling. Stir in the ramen and cook it for 4 to 4 min or until it is done.
6. Spoon the noodles into serving bowl then top it with the sautéed beef. Serve it warm.
7. Enjoy.

Japanese
Dashi Omelet

Prep Time: 15 mins
Total Time: 25 mins

Servings per Recipe: 6
Calories	63 kcal
Fat	3.8 g
Carbohydrates	2.6g
Protein	4.4 g
Cholesterol	124 mg
Sodium	87 mg

Ingredients

4 eggs
1/4 C. prepared dashi stock
1 tbsp white sugar
1 tsp mirin

1/2 tsp soy sauce
1/2 tsp vegetable oil, or more as needed

Directions

1. Get a large mixing bowl: Beat the eggs in it well. Add the dashi stock, sugar, mirin, and soy sauce. Mix them well.
2. Place a large wok over medium heat. Heat the oil in it. Pour enough of the eggs mix to make a thin layer to cover the bottom of the pan.
3. Cook it until it becomes firm from the bottom. Roll the omelet and until you reach the side of the wok and leave it there.
4. Grease the wok again with oil and pour in it another thin layer of the eggs mix. Cook it until it becomes firm and roll it to the side on the first egg roll.
5. Repeat the process with the remaining egg mix until it is all used. Serve your omelet warm.
6. Enjoy.

HAWAIIAN
Ramen Wok

Prep Time: 25 mins
Total Time: 35 mins

Servings per Recipe: 2
Calories   552.7
Fat   38.0g
Cholesterol   61.3mg
Sodium   1944.2mg
Carbohydrates   37.8g
Protein   16.0g

Ingredients

6 oz. Spam
1 green bell pepper, stir fried, chopped
1/2 C. onion, diced
1 (3 oz.) packages ramen noodles
1 clove garlic, peeled and diced
1/4 tsp salt

1/4 tsp ground black pepper
1 tbsp olive oil
1/2 tsp butter

Directions

1. Place a large saucepan over medium heat. Cook in it 2 C. of water until they start boiling.
2. Place in it the noodles without the seasoning packet according to the directions on the package. Drain it and place it aside.
3. Place a large wok over medium heat. Heat in it the butter until it melts with olive oil. Cook in them the onion for 3 min.
4. Stir in the Spam, bell pepper, and the garlic. Cook them for 4 min.
5. Stir in 1/2 C. of the noodles cooking liquid with the drained noodles. Let it sit for 1 min then serve it warm.
6. Enjoy.

Sweet
Ramen with Tofu

🥘 Prep Time: 10 mins

🕐 Total Time: 20 mins

Servings per Recipe: 1

Calories	335.1
Fat	27.8g
Cholesterol	0.0mg
Sodium	33.9mg
Carbohydrates	18.9g
Protein	8.4g

Ingredients

1 package chicken-flavored ramen noodles
2 C. water
2 tbsp vegetable oil
3 slices tofu, 1/4 inch thick
2 C. soy bean sprouts or 2 C. mung bean sprouts
1/2 small zucchini, thinly sliced

2 green onions, sliced
1/2 C. sweet green pea pods
flour
seasoning salt
sesame oil

Directions

1. Slice each tofu piece into 3 chunks. Dust them with some flour.
2. Place a large wok over medium heat. Heat 1 tbsp of oil in it. Cook in it the tofu for 1 to 2 min on each side. Drain it and place it aside.
3. Heat a splash of oil in the same pan. Sauté in it the veggies for 6 min. Place them aside.
4. Cook the noodles by following the directions on the package. Stir in it the seasoning packet.
5. Place a large wok over medium heat. Heat a splash of oil in it. Cook in it the bean sprouts for 1 min.
6. Lay the fried bean sprouts in the bottom of serving bowl. Top it with the ramen, cooked veggies and tofu. Serve them hot.
7. Enjoy.

GINGER
Beef Ramen

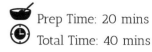

Prep Time: 20 mins
Total Time: 40 mins

Servings per Recipe: 4
Calories	902.3
Fat	42.4g
Cholesterol	68.2mg
Sodium	2750.8mg
Carbohydrates	89.7g
Protein	39.5g

Ingredients

14 oz. dried ramen noodles
12 oz. beef sirloin, half frozen to make
slicing easier
1 1/2 quarts chicken stock
1 inch piece gingerroot, roughly sliced
2 garlic cloves, halved
2 tbsp sake
3 tbsp shoyu, plus
1 tbsp shoyu, for stir-frying

1 bok choy, trimmed and thinly shredded
2 tbsp peanut oil
8 dried shiitake mushrooms, soaked in
warm water for 30 minutes, drained and
thinly sliced
sea salt, to taste
fresh ground black pepper, to taste

Directions

1. Prepare the noodles according to the instructions on the package. Discard the water and place the noodles aside.
2. Slice the beef into thin slices.
3. Place a large saucepan over medium heat. Heat the stock in it. Stir in it the ginger with garlic and cook them for 12 min over low heat.
4. Once the time is up, drain the ginger with garlic and discard them. Add the sake, shoyu and salt and pepper to the broth.
5. Place a large wok over medium heat. Heat 1 tbsp of oil in it. Sauté in it the baby bok choy for 3 min. Drain it and place it aside.
6. Heat the remaining oil in the same wok. Sauté in it the beef with mushroom for 4 min. Stir into them the shoyu with a pinch of salt and pepper.
7. Stir the noodles in some hot water to heat it then drain it. Place it in serving bowls then top it with the beef, shiitake, and bok choy.
8. Pour the chicken broth all over them. Serve it right away.
9. Enjoy.

Louisiana
x Japan Ramen

🍲 Prep Time: 10 mins
🕐 Total Time: 15 mins

Servings per Recipe: 1

Calories	150.2
Fat	12.2g
Cholesterol	94.3mg
Sodium	206.4mg
Carbohydrates	1.2g
Protein	8.8g

Ingredients

1 (3 oz.) packages shrimp flavor ramen noodle soup
6 large shrimp, skin and veins removed
1 tbsp butter
1/4 tsp garlic powder

1 tsp creole seasoning
1/4 tsp black pepper
1/2 tsp hot sauce

Directions

1. Cut the noodles in half and prepare it according to the directions on the package without the seasoning packet.
2. Place a large wok over medium heat. Melt the butter in it. Sauté in it the shrimp with garlic powder, creole seasoning, and black pepper for 6 min.
3. Pour the noodles with 1/4 C. of the cooking liquid in a serving bowl.
4. Top it with the shrimp and hot sauce then serve it warm.
5. Enjoy.

AMERICAN
Ground Beef Ramen

Prep Time: 7 mins
Total Time: 12 mins

Servings per Recipe: 4
Calories	770.2
Fat	29.6g
Cholesterol	77.1mg
Sodium	1849.2mg
Carbohydrates	91.2g
Protein	38.7g

Ingredients

1 lb ground beef, drained
3 (3 oz.) packets beef-flavor ramen noodles
5 C. boiling water
1/4-1/2 C. water
1 (16 oz.) cans corn

1 (16 oz.) cans peas
1/4 C. soy sauce
1/2 tsp ground red pepper
1 dash cinnamon
2 tsp sugar

Directions

1. Place a large wok over medium heat. Heat a splash of oil in it. Add the beef and cook it for 8 min. Place it aside.
2. Place a large saucepan over medium heat. Heat 5 C. of water in it until it starts boiling. Cook in it the noodles for 3 to 4 min.
3. Remove the noodles from the water and stir it into the wok with the beef.
4. Add the water, corn, peas, soy sauce, red pepper, cinnamon, sugar and 1 and a half of the seasoning packets. Toss them to coat.
5. Let them cook for 6 min while stirring often. Serve your ramen Wok Hot.
6. Enjoy.

Tipsy
Japanese Crumbled Beef

Prep Time: 10 mins
Total Time: 16 mins

Servings per Recipe: 4
Calories	232 kcal
Fat	13.2 g
Carbohydrates	7.4g
Protein	14.9 g
Cholesterol	52 mg
Sodium	726 mg

Ingredients

3/4 lb ground beef
2 tbsp freshly grated ginger
3 tbsp soy sauce
3 tbsp sake

2 tbsp mirin
1 tbsp white sugar, or more to taste

Directions

1. Place a large wok over medium heat and heat it. Add the beef and cook it for 8 min.

2. Stir in the remaining ingredients. Cook them until they start boiling. Keep boiling them for 2 min. Serve your crumbled beef warm with some rice.

3. Enjoy.

SAVORY
and Sweet Omelet

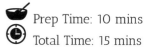 Prep Time: 10 mins
Total Time: 15 mins

Servings per Recipe: 1
Calories	82 kcal
Fat	5 g
Carbohydrates	2.9g
Protein	6.6 g
Cholesterol	186 mg
Sodium	369 mg

Ingredients

1 tbsp water
1 tsp soy sauce, or to taste
1/2 tsp white sugar

1 egg

Directions

1. Get a mixing bowl: Whisk in it the water, soy sauce, and sugar well. Stir in the egg and mix them again.
2. Place a large wok over medium heat. Grease it with a cooking spray. Pour into it the egg mix and spread it in the pan.
3. Cook it for 4 min until it becomes golden brown from the sides. Serve it warm.
4. Enjoy.

Tropical
Curry Ramen

Prep Time: 20 mins
Total Time: 30 mins

Servings per Recipe: 4
Calories	553.2
Fat	25.4g
Cholesterol	0.0mg
Sodium	1466.3mg
Carbohydrates	76.3g
Protein	8.5g

Ingredients

2 (3 oz.) packages ramen noodles
1 tbsp vegetable oil
1 tsp crushed red pepper flakes
2 garlic cloves, minced
1 C. shredded cabbage
1 C. thinly sliced mixed mushrooms
1 C. chopped broccoli
1 tbsp peanut butter
1 tbsp soy sauce
1 tbsp brown sugar

1 C. coconut milk
1 tsp curry powder
1 tsp sambal oelek
1 lime, juice of
1/2 tsp salt
1 tbsp crushed peanuts
1/4 C. chopped cilantro
lime wedge

Directions

1. Prepare the noodles according to the directions on the package without the seasoning packets. Drain the noodles and reserve the cooking liquid.
2. Place a large wok over medium heat. Heat the oil in it. Sauté in it the garlic with red pepper for 40 sec.
3. Stir in the cabbage, mushrooms and broccoli. Add the veggies and cook them for 6 min. Stir the noodles into the wok and place them aside.
4. Place another wok over medium heat. Stir in it the peanut butter, soy sauce, brown sugar, coconut milk, curry powder, sambal oelek and salt. Cook them until they start boiling.
5. Add the cooked noodles and veggies and stir them to coat. Stir in 1/4 C. of the cooking liquid. Cook them until they mix becomes thick.
6. Let the ramen wok rest for 6 min. Top the ramen wok with the cilantro and peanuts then serve them hot.
7. Enjoy.

JAPANESE
Sweet Chicken Stir Fry

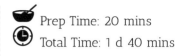

Prep Time: 20 mins
Total Time: 1 d 40 mins

Servings per Recipe: 4

Calories	587 kcal
Fat	32.5 g
Carbohydrates	18g
Protein	48.7 g
Cholesterol	146 mg
Sodium	2545 mg

Ingredients

1 (3 lb) whole chicken, cut into pieces
1 tbsp grated fresh ginger root
1 clove garlic, crushed
3 tbsp white sugar
2/3 C. soy sauce
1 tbsp sake

1/4 C. mirin
2 tbsp cooking oil

Directions

1. Clean the chicken and dry it.
2. Get a glass oven pan: Mix in it the ginger, garlic, sugar, soy sauce, sake and mirin. Add to it the chicken pieces and stir them to coat.
3. Cover the dish with a plastic wrap and place it in the fridge for 2 h to 8 h.
4. Place a large wok over medium heat. Heat the oil in it. Drain the chicken pieces from the marinade and fry them until they become golden brown.
5. Drain the chicken pieces and place them aside. Remove the grease from the wok Pour the marinade from the chicken into the wok with the browned chicken pieces.
6. Lower the heat and put on the lid. Cook the marinade for 9 min to make the sauce. Remove the lid and keep cooking them until the chicken is done and the sauce is thick.
7. Serve your saucy chicken warm.
8. Enjoy.

Japanese
Sesame Egg Sushi

🍳 Prep Time: 30 mins
🕐 Total Time: 55 mins

Servings per Recipe: 6
Calories	218 kcal
Fat	6.7 g
Carbohydrates	33.2g
Protein	6.7 g
Cholesterol	93 mg
Sodium	535 mg

Ingredients

1 C. sushi rice, or Japanese short-grain white rice
3 eggs, beaten
1/4 tsp salt
1 tbsp vegetable oil
3 tbsp rice vinegar

2 tbsp white sugar
1 tsp salt
2 tbsp black sesame seeds
6 sprigs Italian parsley with long stems

Directions

1. Cook the rice according to the directions on the package. Drain and place it aside to lose heat completely.
2. Get a mixing bowl: Mix in it the eggs with 1/4 tsp of salt.
3. Place a large wok over medium heat. Grease it with oil and heat it. Spread in it 1/6 of the beaten eggs then cook them for until it is done.
4. Flip the egg omelet and cook it for 10 sec. Place it aside. Repeat the process with the rest of the mix to make 6 thin omelet.
5. Get a small bowl: Mix in it the vinegar, sugar, and 1 tsp salt. Place it in the microwave and heat for 10 to 15 sec.
6. Stir in the sesame seeds with vinegar.
7. Place an egg omelet on working surface and place in the center of the edge a spoonful of rice. Roll it to make a square then use the Italian parsley to tie it.
8. Serve it with your favorite dip.
9. Enjoy.

$3 DOLLAR
Dinner

 Prep Time: 5 mins

Total Time: 5 mins

Servings per Recipe: 1
Calories	780.9
Fat	27.8g
Cholesterol	30.6mg
Sodium	2388.2mg
Carbohydrates	69.2g
Protein	62.3g

Ingredients

1 (6 oz.) cans tuna in vegetable oil
1 (3 oz.) packets ramen noodles, any
flavor

1/2 C. frozen mixed vegetables

Directions

1. Place a large wok over medium heat. Heat in it a splash of oil. Cook in it the tuna for 2 to 3 min.
2. Prepare the ramen noodles according to the directions on the package with the veggies.
3. Remove the noodles and veggies from the water and transfer them to the pan. Stir into them the seasoning packet and cook them for 2 to 3 min.
4. Serve your ramen tuna warm.
5. Enjoy.

Sweet and Spicy Ramen Stir Fry

Prep Time: 10 mins
Total Time: 30 mins

Servings per Recipe: 4
Calories	585.2
Fat	25.9g
Cholesterol	0.0mg
Sodium	2516.7mg
Carbohydrates	67.4g
Protein	25.1g

Ingredients

1 (14 oz.) packages extra firm tofu, cubed
8 tsp soy sauce
2 tbsp vegetable oil
8 oz. shiitake mushrooms, sliced thin
2 tsp Asian chili sauce
3 garlic cloves, minced
1 tbsp grated fresh ginger
3 1/2 C. low sodium chicken broth

4 (3 oz.) packages ramen noodles, packets discarded
3 tbsp cider vinegar
2 tsp sugar
1 (6 oz.) bags Baby Spinach

Directions

1. Use some paper towels to pat the tofu dry.
2. Get a mixing bowl: Stir in it the tofu with 2 tsp of soy sauce.
3. Place a large wok over medium heat. Heat 1 tbsp of oil in it. Sauté in it the tofu for 2 to 3 min on each side then drain it and place it aside.
4. Heat the rest of the oil in the same wok. Sauté in it the mushroom for 5 min. Add the chili sauce, garlic, and ginger. Let them cook for 40 sec.
5. Crush the ramen into pieces. Stir it into the wok with the broth and cook them for 3 min or until the ramen is done.
6. Add 2 tbsp soy sauce, vinegar, and sugar. Add the spinach and cook them for 2 to 3 min or until it welts.
7. Fold the tofu into the noodles then serve it warm.
8. Enjoy.

RAMEN
Steak Wok

Prep Time: 10 mins
Total Time: 25 mins

Servings per Recipe: 4
Calories	178.8
Fat	8.3g
Cholesterol	0.0mg
Sodium	732.3mg
Carbohydrates	22.1g
Protein	6.0g

Ingredients

1 lb beef round tip steak, stripped
2 cloves garlic, minced
1 tbsp light sesame oil
1/4 tsp ground red pepper
1 (3 oz.) packages ramen noodles
1 (1 lb) package broccoli, carrots and

water chestnuts
1 tsp light sesame oil
1 (4 1/2 oz.) jars mushrooms, drained
1 tbsp soy sauce

Directions

1. Get a mixing bowl: Stir in it the beef strips, garlic, one tbsp sesame oil and ground red pepper.
2. Place a pot over medium heat. Cook in it 2 C. of water until it starts boiling. Crush the noodles into 3 portions.
3. Stir it in the pot with the veggies and cook them until they start boiling. Lower the heat and cook them for an extra 3 min.
4. Pour the mix in a colander to remove the water. Place the noodles and veggies mix back into the pot.
5. Add the seasoning packet and stir them well.
6. Place a large wok over medium heat. Heat 1 tsp of sesame oil in it. Cook in it the beef slices for 4 to 5 min or until they are done.
7. Stir the ramen and veggies mix into the wok with the mushrooms and soy sauce. Cook them for an extra 3 min. Serve your wok warm.
8. Enjoy.

Japanese
Spring Stir Fry

Prep Time: 10 mins
Total Time: 40 mins

Servings per Recipe: 4
Calories   356.5
Fat   7.2g
Cholesterol   104.4mg
Sodium   616.0mg
Carbohydrates   60.6g
Protein   10.5g

Ingredients

4 C. cooked rice or 1 C. uncooked rice
1 C. frozen peas, thawed
2 tbsp carrots, finely diced
2 eggs, beaten
1/2 C. onion, diced
1 1/2 tbsp butter

2 tbsp soy sauce
salt
pepper

Directions

1. Prepare the rice according to the directions on the package. Drain the rice and place it in the fridge to lose heat.
2. Place a large greased wok over medium heat. Scramble in it the eggs while crumbling them then place them aside.
3. Get a large mixing bowl: Place in it the rice with scrambled eggs, peas, grated carrot, scrambled egg and diced onion. Mix them well.
4. Place a large wok over medium heat. Heat the butter in it until it melts. Add the rice mix with soy sauce, a pinch of salt and pepper.
5. Stir fry it for 9 min. Serve your stir fried rice warm.
6. Enjoy.

JAPANESE
Fruity Chicken Curry

Prep Time: 10 mins
Total Time: 55 mins

Servings per Recipe: 4	
Calories	420.5
Fat	17.9g
Cholesterol	101.1mg
Sodium	734.0mg
Carbohydrates	33.1g
Protein	31.9g

Ingredients

3 C. chicken stock
1 tbsp canola oil
1 lb boneless skinless chicken, cut into chunks
salt and pepper
3 tbsp butter
1 tsp fresh ginger, finely chopped
1/2 medium onion, finely chopped
1/2 medium onion, cut into 1-inch chunks
1 garlic clove, finely chopped
3 tbsp flour
2 tbsp curry powder
2 tbsp crushed tomatoes
1 bay leaf
1 medium carrot, chopped to 1/2-inch pieces
1 medium potato, chopped in 1-inch pieces
1 small fuji apple, grated
1 tsp honey
1 tbsp soy sauce

Directions

1. Place a medium saucepan over medium heat: Pour the stock in it and heat it through. Sprinkle some salt and pepper on the chicken.

2. Place a large wok over medium heat: Heat the oil in it.

3. Add the chicken pieces and cook them for 5 min on each side. Drain it and place it aside.

4. Add the butter to the wok and heat it until it melts. Cook in it the ginger, garlic, and chopped onion for 4 min.

5. Add the flour and cook them for 2 min. Stir in 1/2 C. of hot stock and mix them well. Stir in the tomato with curry.

6. Transfer the mix to the pot with the remaining hot stock. Stir in the chicken, onion, potato, and carrot.

7. Cook the curry until it starts simmering. Cook it for 32 min. Stir in the apples, soy sauce, and honey.

8. Cook the curry for 6 min. Serve it warm with some rice.

9. Enjoy.

Ramen Green Bean Stir Fry

🥄 Prep Time: 7 mins
🕐 Total Time: 27 mins

Servings per Recipe: 6	
Calories	370.9
Fat	27.2g
Cholesterol	0.0mg
Sodium	338.3mg
Carbohydrates	28.2g
Protein	6.4g

Ingredients

1 1/2 lbs fresh green beans
2 (3 oz.) packages ramen noodles
1/2 C. vegetable oil
1/3 C. toasted almond

salt, as needed
black pepper, as needed

Directions

1. Trim the green beans and slice them into 3 to 4 inches pieces.
2. Place the green beans in a steamer and cook them until they become soft.
3. Get a large wok. Stir in it the oil with 1 seasoning packet.
4. Crush 1 packet of noodles and stir it into the wok. Add the steamed green beans and cook them for 3 to 4 min.
5. Adjust the seasoning of your stir fry then serve it warm.
6. Enjoy.

JAPANESE
Chicken Thighs Wok

Prep Time: 10 mins
Total Time: 30 mins

Servings per Recipe: 4
Calories	128.4
Fat	7.2g
Cholesterol	39.4mg
Sodium	585.9mg
Carbohydrates	6.1g
Protein	9.6g

Ingredients

2 - 3 boneless chicken thighs
8 fresh shiitake mushrooms
8 shishito green peppers or 3 small bell peppers
2 - 3 tbsp mirin
2 - 3 tbsp soy sauce

japanese sansho pepper (optional)
shichimi togarashi pepper or red chili pepper flakes (optional)

Directions

1. Discard the fat from the chicken. Discard the mushroom tips and cut them into quarters.
2. Remove the bell peppers stems and cut them into bite size pieces.
3. Place a large wok over medium heat. Grease it with some oil. Cook in it the chicken thighs with the skin facing down until it becomes crisp and golden brown.
4. Stir in the pepper with mushroom. Flip the chicken thighs and cook them on the other side until they become golden brown.
5. Stir in the mirin with soy sauce. Cook them until they sauce becomes thick, the chicken and veggies done. Serve your chicken wok warm.
6. Enjoy.

Apple
Ramen Salad

Prep Time: 15 mins
Total Time: 20 mins

Servings per Recipe: 10
Calories	343.1
Fat	28.5g
Cholesterol	9.1mg
Sodium	235.0mg
Carbohydrates	19.8g
Protein	4.0g

Ingredients

12 oz. broccoli florets
1 (12 oz.) bags broccoli coleslaw mix
1/4 C. sunflower seeds
2 (3 oz.) packages ramen noodles
3 tbsp butter
2 tbsp olive oil
1/4 C. sliced almonds

3/4 C. vegetable oil
1/4 C. brown sugar
1/4 C. apple cider vinegar
1/4 C. green onion, chopped

Directions

1. Place a large wok over medium heat. Heat the oil in it.
2. Press your ramen with your hands to crush it. Stir it in the wok with the almonds.
3. Cook them for 6 min then place the wok aside.
4. Get a large mixing bowl: Toss in it the broccoli, broccoli slaw and sunflowers. Add the noodles mix and toss them again.
5. Get a small mixing bowl: Combine in it the vegetable oil, brown sugar, apple cider vinegar and the Ramen noodle seasoning packet to make the vinaigrette.
6. Drizzle the vinaigrette all over the salad and stir it to coat. Serve your salad with the green onions on top.
7. Enjoy

MUNG BANG
Noodles Wok

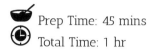 Prep Time: 45 mins
Total Time: 1 hr

Servings per Recipe: 6
Calories	378.5
Fat	16.0g
Cholesterol	54.5mg
Sodium	1082.0mg
Carbohydrates	36.5g
Protein	23.9g

Ingredients

1 lb lean ground beef, cooked
6 slices turkey bacon, chopped
2 (3 oz.) packages ramen noodles
3 garlic cloves, minced
1 medium red onion, diced
1 medium cabbage, chopped
3 carrots, cut into thin 1 inch strips
1 red bell pepper, cut into bite size
pieces

2-4 tbsp light soy sauce
3 C. bean sprouts
light soy sauce, to taste
crushed red pepper flakes

Directions

1. Place a large wok over medium heat.
2. Cook in it the bacon until it becomes crisp. Drain it and place it aside. Keep about 2 tbsp of the bacon grease in the pan.
3. Sauté in it the garlic with onion for 4 min. Stir in 2 tbsp of soy sauce and the carrots.
4. Let them cook for 3 min. Stir in the bell pepper with cabbage and let them cook for an extra 7 min.
5. Cook the noodles according to the manufacturer's directions. Drain it and stir it with a splash of olive oil.
6. Stir the beef, bacon and crushed red pepper flakes into the wok with the cooked veggies. Let them cook for 4 min while stirring often.
7. Once the time is up, stir the bean sprouts and Ramen noodles into the veggies mix. Let them cook for an extra 3 min while stirring all the time.
8. Serve your noodles wok warm with some hot sauce.
9. Enjoy.

Hawaiian
Fried Rice II

🥣 Prep Time: 15 mins
🕐 Total Time: 40 mins

Servings per Recipe: 8
Calories   532.0
Fat   5.0g
Cholesterol   139.5mg
Sodium   2222.7mg
Carbohydrates   102.6g
Protein   17.5g

Ingredients

4 1/2 C. dry rice, cooked and cooled
6 -7 eggs, with a splash water, scrambled
1 (11 oz.) cans Spam lite, diced
1 yellow onion, diced
12 oz. frozen peas and carrots, thawed
Glaze
1 C. aloha shoyu soy sauce

6 -7 tbsp for Kikkoman soy sauce
4 -5 garlic cloves, minced
2 tbsp oyster sauce
1 tsp sesame oil

Directions

1. In a wok, heat 1/2 tbsp of the vegetable oil on medium-high heat and cook the eggs till scrambled.
2. Transfer the scrambled eggs into a bowl.
3. In the same wok, heat 1 tbsp of the oil on medium-high heat and sauté the onions and Spam till golden and starts to crisp.
4. Meanwhile in a bowl, add all the sauce ingredients and stir till the sugar dissolves.
5. Stir in the thawed peas, carrots and sauce mixture and bring to a boil on high heat.
6. Cook till the mixture changes into a glaze.
7. Slowly, add the cooled rice and eggs, breaking up any clumps of rice and cook till heated completely.
8. Serve immediately.

FRIED
Rice Cauliflower

Prep Time: 15 mins
Total Time: 45 mins

Servings per Recipe: 6
Calories	366 kcal
Fat	19.2 g
Carbohydrates	15.8g
Protein	33.3 g
Cholesterol	132 mg
Sodium	1065 mg

Ingredients

2 C. frozen peas
1/2 C. water
1/4 C. sesame oil, divided
4 C. cubed beef loin
6 green onions, sliced
1 large carrot, cubed

2 cloves garlic, minced
20 oz. shredded cauliflower
6 tbsp soy sauce
2 eggs, beaten

Directions

1. In a pan, add the peas and water and bring to a boil.
2. Reduce the heat to medium-low and cook for about 5 minutes.
3. Drain the peas completely.
4. In a wok, heat 2 tbsp of the sesame oil on medium-high heat and sear the beef for about 7-10 minutes.
5. Transfer the beef into a plate.
6. In the same wok, heat the remaining 2 tbsp of the sesame oil and sauté the green onions, carrot and garlic for about 5 minutes.
7. Stir in the cauliflower and cook for about 4-5 minutes.
8. Stir in the beef, peas and and soy sauce and stir fry for about 3-5 minutes.
9. Push the beef mixture to one side of the wok.
10. Add the beaten eggs and cook for about 3-5 minutes, stirring continuously.
11. Stir the cooked eggs into the beef mixture, breaking up any large chunks.
12. Serve hot.

Curried
Apple and Raisins Fried Rice

Prep Time: 30 mins
Total Time: 55 mins

Servings per Recipe: 4

Calories	248 kcal
Fat	5.6 g
Carbohydrates	37.5g
Protein	12.7 g
Cholesterol	110 mg
Sodium	371 mg

Ingredients

6 oz. shrimp - peeled, veined, and cut into 1-inch pieces
1 pinch salt and ground black pepper
1 tsp cornstarch
1 tbsp vegetable oil
1 tsp minced garlic
1 egg, beaten
1 C. diced button mushrooms
3/4 C. frozen mixed vegetables

1 apple - peeled, cored, and diced
2 tbsp raisins
1 tsp curry powder
1 tbsp light soy sauce
2 C. overnight steamed white rice
1 green onion, diced

Directions

1. In a bowl, mix together the shrimp, salt, pepper and cornstarch.
2. In a wok, heat the oil on medium heat and cook the shrimp mixture for about 5 minutes.
3. Transfer the shrimp mixture into a plate.
4. In the same wok, add the garlic and sauté for about 1 minute.
5. Add he egg and cook for about 3 minutes, stirring continuously.
6. Stir in the mushrooms and cook for about 5 minutes.
7. Stir in the mixed vegetables and cook for about 3-5 minutes.
8. Stir in the apple, raisins and curry powder and cook for about 3 minutes.
9. Stir in the rice, soy sauce, salt and pepper and cook for about 3-5 minutes.
10. Stir in the shrimp mixture and green onion and cook for about 2-4 minutes.

SEAFOOD
Sampler Fried Rice

Prep Time: 15 mins
Total Time: 55 mins

Servings per Recipe: 4

Calories	304 kcal
Fat	12.2 g
Carbohydrates	37.4g
Protein	11.6 g
Cholesterol	68 mg
Sodium	1294 mg

Ingredients

2/3 C. uncooked long grain white rice
1 1/3 C. water
3 tbsp vegetable oil
2 medium onions, cut into wedges
3 cloves garlic, chopped
1/2 tbsp white sugar
2 tsp salt
1 egg, beaten

1/4 lb. cooked crab meat
3 green onions, chopped
1 tbsp chopped cilantro
1/2 cucumber, sliced
1 lime, sliced

Directions

1. In a pan, add the rice and water and bring to a boil.
2. Reduce the heat and simmer, covered for about 20 minutes.
3. In a wok, heat the oil on medium heat and sauté the onions and garlic till tender.
4. Stir in the rice, sugar and salt and cook for about 5 minutes.
5. Stir in the egg and increase the heat to high.
6. Stir in the crab meat, green onions and cilantro and cook for about 2-5 minutes.
7. Serve with a garnishing of the cucumber and lime slices.

Creamy
Corn Soup

🥣 Prep Time: 10 mins
🕐 Total Time: 50 mins

Servings per Recipe: 6
Calories	157 kcal
Fat	3.3 g
Carbohydrates	16.2g
Protein	16 g
Cholesterol	26 mg
Sodium	1052 mg

Ingredients

1/2 lb skinless, boneless chicken breast meat - finely diced
1 tbsp sherry
1/4 tsp salt
2 egg whites
1 (14.75 oz.) can cream-style corn
4 C. chicken broth
2 tsps soy sauce

1/4 C. water
2 tbsps cornstarch
4 slices crisp cooked bacon, crumbled

Directions

1. Get a bowl, combine: chicken, egg whites, sherry, and salt.
2. Combine in the cream corn and continue mixing everything until it's smooth.
3. Now get the following boiling in a wok: soy sauce and chicken broth.
4. Combine in the chicken mix and get everything boiling again.
5. Now set the heat to low, and cook the soup for 5 mins while stirring.
6. Combine some cornstarch and water then pour this mix into your boiling soup and keep stirring everything for 3 more mins. Then add in your bacon and serve. Enjoy.

GINGER
Chili Plum Steak

Prep Time: 10 mins
Total Time: 20 mins

Servings per Recipe: 4
Calories	550.3
Fat	30.3g
Cholesterol	140.7mg
Sodium	778.6mg
Carbohydrates	26.6g
Protein	40.1g

Ingredients

1.5 lbs rump steak
2/3 C. plum sauce
1 tbsp soy sauce
1 garlic clove, crushed
1 tsp fresh ginger, grated
1/2 tsp fresh red chili, chopped
2 tsp sugar
2 tsp dry sherry

2 tsp corn flour
2 tbsp oil
2 tsp corn flour, extra
½ C. water
1 small beef stock cube, crumbled

Directions

1. Trim the steak and slice thinly.
2. In a large bowl, mix together the steak slices, sauces, garlic, ginger, red chili, sugar, sherry and corn flour.
3. Refrigerate, covered to marinate for at least 30 minutes or overnight.
4. Remove the steak slices from the bowl and reserve the marinade.
5. In a wok, heat a little oil and stir fry the steak slices in batches till browned.
6. In a small bowl, dissolve the extra corn flour with water.
7. In the wok or skillet, add all steak slices, reserved marinade, corn flour mixture and stock cube and bring to a boil, stirring continuously.
8. Boil till the mixture thickens.
9. Serve with the rice.

Beef
and Broccoli I

Prep Time: 10 mins
Total Time: 1 hr 10 mins

Servings per Recipe: 4
Calories   665 kcal
Carbohydrates   104.6 g
Cholesterol   39 mg
Fat   13.8 g
Protein   30.5 g
Sodium   1594 mg

Ingredients

2 cups brown rice
4 cups water
2 tbsps cornstarch
2 tsps white sugar
6 tbsps soy sauce
1/4 cup white wine
1 tbsp minced fresh ginger
1 pound boneless beef round steak, cut into thin strips
1 tbsp vegetable oil
3 cups broccoli florets

2 carrots, thinly sliced
1 (6 ounce) package frozen pea pods, thawed
2 tbsps chopped onion
1 (8 ounce) can sliced water chestnuts, undrained
1 cup Chinese cabbage
2 large heads bok choy, chopped
1 tbsp vegetable oil

Directions

1. Get your rice boiling in water, set the heat to low, cover the pan, and let the rice cook for 40 mins until done.
2. Get a bowl, combine the following ingredients: soy sauce, cornstarch, wine, and sugar.
3. Mix everything evenly then add the ginger and beef to the marinade.
4. Get a wok and heat 1 tsp oil.
5. Begin to stir fry for 1 min: onions, broccoli, pea pods, and carrots.
6. Mix in: bok choy, Chinese cabbage, and the water chestnuts.
7. Place a lid on the pan and let everything fry for 4 mins.
8. Now remove everything from the pan and add in 1 tsp oil.
9. Begin to fry the beef for 4 mins. Then add the veggies back into the mix and continue frying everything for 3 more mins.
10. Enjoy with cooked brown rice.

PINEAPPLE
Pepper Curry

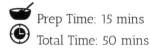

Prep Time: 15 mins
Total Time: 50 mins

Servings per Recipe: 6

Calories	623 kcal
Fat	34.5 g
Carbohydrates	77.5g
Protein	20.3 g
Cholesterol	20 mg
Sodium	781 mg

Ingredients

2 C. uncooked jasmine rice
1 quart water
1/4 C. red curry paste, see appendix
2 (13.5 oz.) cans coconut milk
2 skinless, boneless chicken breast
halves - cut into thin strips
3 tbsp fish sauce
1/4 C. white sugar

1 1/2 C. sliced bamboo shoots, drained
1/2 red bell pepper, julienned
1/2 green bell pepper, julienned
1/2 small onion, chopped
1 C. pineapple chunks, drained

Directions

1. In a pan, add the rice and water and bring to a boil.
2. Reduce the heat to low and simmer, covered for about 25 minutes.
3. In a bowl, add the curry paste and 1 can of the coconut milk and beat till well combined.
4. Transfer the curry paste mixture into a wok.
5. Add the remaining coconut milk, chicken, fish sauce, sugar, and bamboo shoots and bring to a boil.
6. Cook for about 15 minutes, stirring occasionally.
7. Stir in the bell peppers and onion and cook for about 10 minutes.
8. Remove from the heat and immediately, stir in the pineapple.
9. Serve over the cooked rice.

Halibut
BBQ Tacos

Prep Time: 15 mins
Total Time: 25 mins

Servings per Recipe: 4
Calories	428.4
Fat	10.3g
Cholesterol	109.6mg
Sodium	838.7mg
Carbohydrates	36.3g
Protein	44.7g

Ingredients

1 1/2 lbs halibut fillets, chunks
2-3 tbsp cajun seasoning
2 C. shredded green cabbage
1 C. shredded red cabbage
1/4 C. cider vinegar
1/4 C. sour cream
6 green onions, chopped

1/2-1 tsp salt
8 flour tortillas
lemon wedge
salsa
tartar sauce
guacamole

Directions

1. Before you do anything, preheat the grill.
2. Get a mixing bowl: Stir in it the halibut fish with Cajun seasoning.
3. Get a grilling wok and grease it with some oil. Place in it the halibut fish then cook it over the hot coals for 9 to 12 min.
4. Get a small mixing bowl: Whisk in it the vinegar, sour cream, green onions, and salt. Stir in the cabbage.
5. Add them to the halibut mix and toss them to coat. Divide the mixture between the taco shells then top them with the halibut chunks.
6. Serve your tacos with your favorite toppings.
7. Enjoy.

CHICKEN
Tikka Masala

Prep Time: 30 mins
Total Time: 2 hrs 20 mins

Servings per Recipe: 4

Calories	404 kcal
Carbohydrates	13.3 g
Cholesterol	143 mg
Fat	28.9 g
Protein	24.6 g
Sodium	4499 mg

Ingredients

1 cup yogurt
1 tbsp lemon juice
2 tsps ground cumin
1 tsp ground cinnamon
2 tsps cayenne pepper
2 tsps freshly ground black pepper
1 tbsp minced fresh ginger
4 tsps salt, or to taste
3 boneless skinless chicken breasts, cut into bite-size pieces
4 long skewers

1tbsp butter
1 clove garlic, minced
1 jalapeno pepper, finely chopped
2 tsps ground cumin
2 tsps paprika
3 tsps salt, or to taste
1(8 ounce) can tomato sauce
1 cup heavy cream
1/4 cup chopped fresh cilantro

Directions

1. Take lemon juice, yogurt, two tsps cumin, cayenne, cinnamon, ginger, black pepper, 4 tsps of salt and add into one mixing dish (possibly a big bowl).

2. Add the chicken to the marinade, cover it, and place it in a refrigerator for one hour. Preheat a grill or frying pan to its highest heat.

3. Add chicken to skewers and throw away the marinade.

4. Add some butter or nonstick spray to your grilling grate.

5. Place the chicken on the grill and allow it to cook until its juices are clear. The approx. time is equal to about 5 minutes on each side.

6. Take your butter and place it into a big skillet or wok. The skillet or wok should be placed over medium heat.

7. For about one minute stir fry (sauté) some garlic and jalapeno.

8. Take some paprika and cumin (approx. 2 tbsps each), and also three tsps of salt and add these ingredients to the garlic and jalapeno.

9. Grab some cream and tomato sauce and place the two ingredients on low heat and continually stir the contents until they become thick. This process should take about 20 minutes.

10. Combine everything with your grilled chicken and let everything cook for an additional ten minutes.

11. Plate your contents and add some cilantro as a garnish. Enjoy.

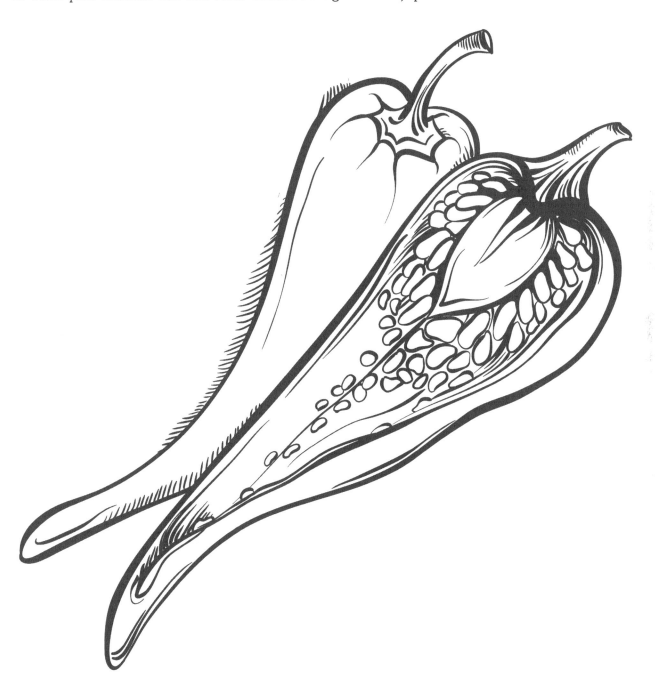

GARLIC
and Lime Shrimp Wok

Prep Time: 10 mins
Total Time: 30 mins

Servings per Recipe: 4
Calories   239.9
Fat   8.7g
Cholesterol   214.3mg
Sodium   2707.8mg
Carbohydrates   16.8g
Protein   23.3g

Ingredients

1/2 C. lime juice
1/4 C. sugar
1 tbsp salt
2 tbsp canola oil
1 tsp minced garlic

1/2 tsp crushed red pepper flakes
1 1/2 lb. peeled shrimp
minced cilantro

Directions

1. In a bowl, add the sugar, lime juice and salt and mix well.
2. In a wok, heat the oil over high heat and cook the garlic and chili flakes for about 40-60 seconds.
3. Stir in the sugar mixture and cook for about 4-5 minutes.
4. Add the shrimp and cook for about 3 minutes, without stirring.
5. Now, cook for about 3 minutes, mixing often
6. Enjoy with a garnishing of the cilantro.

Pan Seared
Halibut Cambodia

🥄 Prep Time: 15 mins
🕐 Total Time: 40 mins

Servings per Recipe: 6
Calories   365.9
Fat   7.1g
Cholesterol   136.2mg
Sodium   1607.8mg
Carbohydrates   19.9g
Protein   53.2g

Ingredients

3/4 C. chopped shallot
1 tbsp olive oil
1/4 C. sugar
1/4 C. Asian fish sauce
1/4 C. water
1 1/2 tsp ground black pepper

2 lb. halibut fillets, cut into pieces
4 scallions, sliced
1/2 bunch cilantro, chopped

Directions

1. In a wok, add the oil over medium heat and cook until heated.
2. Stir in the shallots and cook for about 8-9 minutes, mixing often.
3. With a slotted spoon, place the shallots into a bowl.
4. In the same wok, add the fish sauce, sugar and water over medium heat and cook for about 4 minutes.
5. Add the cooked shallot and black pepper and cook for about 1-2 minutes.
6. Stir in the fish and cook for about 9-10 minutes, flipping after every 3 minutes.
7. Stir in the cilantro and scallions and enjoy.

PINK
and Green Stir Fry

Prep Time: 15 mins
Total Time: 25 mins

Servings per Recipe: 4
Calories	202.5
Fat	8.2g
Cholesterol	142.8mg
Sodium	1073.8mg
Carbohydrates	14.5g
Protein	18.7g

Ingredients

1 lb. shrimp, peeled and de-veined
1/2 tsp salt
1/4 tsp ground black pepper
2 tbsp water
1 tbsp sugar
1 tbsp oyster sauce
1 tbsp cornstarch
2 tbsp vegetable oil

2 garlic cloves, minced
1 onion, sliced
1 lb. asparagus, chopped
1 green onion, chopped

Directions

1. In a bowl, add the shrimp, salt and black pepper and mix well and keep aside.
2. In another bowl, add the sugar, cornstarch, oyster sauce and water and mix until well combined.
3. In a wok, add the oil over high heat and cook until heated through.
4. Add the shrimp, onion and garlic and cook for about 3-4 minutes.
5. Add the asparagus and stir to combine.
6. Add the cornstarch mixture and mix well.
7. Cook until desired thickness of the sauce.
8. Stir in the green onion and remove from the heat.
9. Enjoy hot.

Catfish Skillet

Prep Time: 15 mins
Total Time: 35 mins

Servings per Recipe: 4
Calories	270.6
Fat	14.0g
Cholesterol	62.3mg
Sodium	1203.5mg
Carbohydrates	16.2g
Protein	20.0g

Ingredients

2 tbsp vegetable oil
1/2 lb. peeled matchstick cut ginger
4 (4 oz.) catfish fillets
2 tbsp fish sauce
1 tbsp soy sauce
1 tbsp oyster sauce

1 large yellow onion, sliced
1/4 red bell pepper, cut into matchsticks
1/2 bunch green onion, chopped

Directions

1. In a wok, add the oil over medium heat and cook until heated through.
2. Add the ginger and cook for about 6-7 minutes, stirring frequently.
3. Add the catfish fillets and cook for about 6 minutes, flipping once half way through.
4. With a slotted spoon, transfer the fillets onto a plate and keep aside.
5. In the same wok, add the oyster sauce, fish sauce and soy sauce and stir to combine.
6. Add the bell pepper and onion and cook for about 5 minutes.
7. Add the cooked catfish fillets and place the sauce over the fillets evenly
8. Cook for about 3 minutes
9. Enjoy with a garnishing of the green onions.

EGGPLANTS
in Ginger Vinaigrette Glaze

🥘 Prep Time: 20 mins
🕐 Total Time: 35 mins

Servings per Recipe: 4
Calories   98.5
Fat   0.3g
Cholesterol   0.0mg
Sodium   1012.1mg
Carbohydrates   21.3g
Protein   3.5g

Ingredients

1 large eggplant, cut stem end and dice
4 tbsp soy sauce
3 tbsp sugar
1/4 C. distilled white vinegar
1/4 C. water
1 tbsp dry sherry
1 tsp crushed dried red pepper
6 slices ginger, about the size and

thickness of a quarter
4 scallions, chopped, separate white and
green parts
1 tbsp cornstarch, combined with
2 tbsp water

Directions

1. In a colander, place the eggplant and sprinkle with the salt.
2. Keep aside to drain for about 15 minutes.
3. With your hands, squeeze the liquid.
4. In a small bowl, add the sugar, soy sauce, vinegar and water and mix well.
5. In a wok, add 1 tbsp of the dry sherry and cook until heated.
6. Add the white part of scallion, ginger and red pepper and sauté slightly.
7. Add the squeezed eggplant and cook for about 9-10 minutes, mixing often.
8. Add the sugar mixture over high heat and cook for about 5 minutes.
9. In a bowl, dissolve the cornstarch in water.
10. In the wok, add the cornstarch mixture and green part of scallions and cook until desired thickness of the sauce.
11. Enjoy hot.

Hot and Spicy
Seafood Filets

Prep Time: 15 mins
Total Time: 25 mins

Servings per Recipe: 6
Calories	94.6
Fat	7.0g
Cholesterol	0.0mg
Sodium	477.0mg
Carbohydrates	7.6g
Protein	1.3g

Ingredients

1 tbsp vegetable oil
fish (white fillet)
salt and pepper
2 tbsp vegetable oil
4 shallots, peeled and sliced
2 garlic cloves, chopped
1 - 2 Thai red chili pepper, cut in half
1 1/2 inches piece ginger, peeled and julienned
20 cherry tomatoes, cut in half

2 tbsp fish sauce
2 tbsp rice wine vinegar
6 tbsp water
2 tsp sugar
1 tsp paprika
1 tsp cornstarch
cilantro leaf

Directions

1. In a bowl, add the vinegar, fish sauce, water, cornstarch, sugar and paprika and mi until well combined.
2. Season the fish with the salt and black pepper evenly.
3. In a cast iron skillet, add 1 tbsp of the oil over medium heat and cook until heated through.
4. Add the fish and cook until half done from both sides.
5. Meanwhile, in a wok, add 2 tbsp of the oil and cook until heated through.
6. Add the shallots and stir fry for about 30 seconds.
7. Add the tomatoes and cook for about 4 minutes, mixing occasionally.
8. Add the vinegar mixture and cook for about 1 minute.
9. Transfer the fish onto a platter and top with the vegetable sauce mixture.
10. Enjoy with a garnishing of the cilantro.

KHMER
Shrimp Wok

Prep Time: 15 mins
Total Time: 25 mins

Servings per Recipe: 2
Calories	305.8
Fat	15.1g
Cholesterol	142.8mg
Sodium	1411.5mg
Carbohydrates	25.0g
Protein	18.8g

Ingredients

1/2 C. water
1 tbsp oyster sauce
1 tbsp soy sauce
1 tbsp sugar
1 tbsp cornstarch
2 tbsp vegetable oil
2 garlic cloves, minced
1 onion, sliced

1/2 lb. shrimp, peeled and de-veined
2 large green tomatoes, sliced
1/4 tsp ground black pepper

Directions

1. In a bowl, add the sugar, cornstarch, soy sauce, oyster sauce and water and mix well.
2. Keep aside.
3. In a large wok, add the oil over high heat and cook until heated.
4. Add the shrimp, onion, green tomato and garlic and stir to combine.
5. Add the cornstarch mixture and stir to combine well.
6. Cook until desired doneness of shrimp, mixing frequently.
7. Stir in the pepper and enjoy hot.

Apricot
and Asparagus Wok

Prep Time: 25 mins
Total Time: 40 mins

Servings per Recipe: 4
Calories   582.6
Fat   35.8g
Cholesterol   137.7mg
Sodium   648.6mg
Carbohydrates   22.5g
Protein   46.4g

Ingredients

1 1/2 lb. New York strip steaks, trimmed
2 tbsp soy sauce
1 tbsp ginger, grated
1 garlic clove, large, pressed
1 tbsp dry sherry
1 1/2 tsp apricot preserves, no sugar added
1 1/2 tsp sesame oil

1/4 tsp Chinese five spice powder
4 tsp canola oil
24 asparagus, spears, trimmed
2 tbsp sesame seeds
24 cherry tomatoes

Directions

1. Cut the steaks into slices crosswise.
2. For the marinade: in a re-sealable plastic bag, add all the ingredients.
3. Add the beef and seal the bag.
4. Shake the bag to mix well.
5. Place in the fridge for about 3-4 hours.
6. In a nonstick wok, add 1 tsp of the oil over high heat and cook until heated through.
7. Add 1/3 of the beef and cook for about 2 minutes.
8. With a slotted spoon, transfer the beef into a bowl.
9. Repeat with the remaining beef and 2 tsp of the oil.
10. In the same skillet, add remaining tsp of the oil and cook until heated.
11. Add the asparagus and sesame seeds and sauté for about 4 minutes.
12. Add the tomatoes and cook until heated completely.
13. Transfer the vegetables into the bowl with the steak and toss to coat well.
14. Enjoy.

CAMBODIAN
Breakfast Frittatas

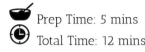

Prep Time: 5 mins
Total Time: 12 mins

Servings per Recipe: 2
Calories   209.5
Fat   423.0mg
Cholesterol   431.8mg
Sodium   1.3g
Carbohydrates   12.7g

Ingredients

4 eggs
1 green onion, chopped
1/4 tsp salt
1/4 tsp msg
black pepper

1 tbsp vegetable oil
2 sweet Chinese sausage

Directions

1. In a bowl, add the eggs, green onion, MSG, salt and black pepper and beat slightly until well combined.

2. In a non-stick wok, add the oil and cook until heated.

3. Add the sausage and cook for about 2 minutes.

4. Drain the grease from the wok.

5. Add the egg mixture and cook for about 3 minutes per side.

6. Enjoy hot.

ENJOY THE RECIPES?

KEEP ON COOKING
WITH 6 MORE FREE COOKBOOKS!

Visit our website and simply enter your email address to join the club and receive your 6 cookbooks.

http://booksumo.com/magnet

 https://www.instagram.com/booksumopress/

https://www.facebook.com/booksumo/

Printed in Great Britain
by Amazon